ECHOES OF THE PAST:

MY DIRT ROAD DIARY

12-7-19

AMY PENNINGTON BRUDNICKI

To Kathy Jo - one of my
best friends in the world -
I hope you enjoy my
Echoes of the Past. I hope
they'll inspire you to write
your own! !!

Happy Reading

BRUDNICKI-PENN PUBLISHING

Amy Pennington Brudnicki

Cover Art by Amy Pennington Brudnicki

Editor Tracy Stephen

This book is a work of non-fiction. Names, characters, places, brands, media, and incidents are factual. The author acknowledges the trademarked status and trademark owners of various products referenced in this work of non-fiction, which have been used without permission. The publication/use of these trademarks are not authorized, associated with, or sponsored by the trademark owners. Any resemblance to actual events, locals, or persons, living or dead, is the cold hard truth.

First Edition, 2019

DEDICATION

To Bru and Tyler, Mom and Clay, Bub and Kim, and all my littles—thank you all for a lifetime of memories . . .

CONTENTS

ABOUT THE COVER . . .

The cover photo is a picture of my little Mammaw, taken in the 1940s when she attended Cumberland College. I've always loved this photo of her. She looked elegant and so very beautiful.

Sometime after I started writing my stories in 2007, I printed off all I had at the time and mailed them to Mammaw in a manilla envelope. She said anytime she was feeling sad or blue, she'd just reach for her envelope and pull out one of my "little stories." She said it so often, I got in the habit of calling them "my little stories."

Back to the cover . . . For years, everyone viewed the shaded area of the picture as a flaw. That's a good lesson in life. What one person views as an imperfection, another person will appreciate or use to his or her advantage. The shaded area was a perfect fit for my title.

I think Mammaw would be proud of me. Little did she know that she'd play such an instrumental part in this book by appearing in so many passages.

Back when I was growing up, she introduced me to Dick & Jane in her one-room schoolhouse. It's funny how life comes full circle sometimes. Back in those carefree days, she taught us the importance of education, of living a good life, and being good little humans. She would've thought I was a *weird little human* for using that phrase. And, you know what? Sometimes, I *am* a weird little human. And that's exactly ok.

My point is, sometimes you plant seeds in people and never know what'll come to fruition. I credit Mammaw for so much of who I am. She was a funny lady and always up for a prank or a good joke. Her phrases come out of me often. Even her cooking comes out of me, but not as often or as well as any of us would like!

I couldn't think of a more perfect image to grace the cover of this collection of memories, my little stories, than one of my little Mammaw.

INTRODUCTION

Echoes of the Past: My Dirt Road Diary is a collection of short stories and blurbs about my life. Some are straight up shenanigans, others are purely nostalgic—and then there's a few that come straight from my soul. These are stories that, long after I'm gone, I'd like my family and friends to remember. And maybe just as importantly, they will be a gift to myself one day when my mind gets tired.

One of my goals in sharing my stories is to help prompt memories in you to share your own. You never know who'd love to hear them.

I'm a fun loving gal who can find humor in almost anything, and it's a good thing since I've always had a knack for getting myself into predicaments.

I'm originally from Hyden, a small town in southeastern Kentucky. I grew up in a holler. Yes, I said, "holler." If I were caught calling it a "Hollow," I'd have to cut my own switch! If you're from Appalachia, you know what that means.

Hurricane Creek is the holler I grew up in. Even though it's just a dot on the map, the memories I took from there are so vast, they simply cannot be measured.

Even though I titled this a diary, I chose to list them randomly, not in chronological order. They're funny, reflective, and often times sentimental. Will they change your life? No, no, they won't. But maybe, just maybe, they'll help brighten your day when you get a glimpse at my forty-six years of light-hearted fun.

Take a walk with me back to the 1970s. That's where we'll start . . .

EPIGRAPH

I'm glad my memories include some old dirt road. Those pathways signify something simple and pure. Like life, they represent a mixed bag of possibilities. Sometimes they're smooth; sometimes they're bumpy; and sometimes they're broken beyond repair. It is what it is. They lead to new discoveries, old treasures, or, quite frankly, to nowhere at all. Sometimes we lose our way, but if we take a moment to just pause, we might discover that that journey can sometimes soothe our souls as we meander back to the path we intended.

Every dirt road I've ever stepped foot on has left a lasting memory on my heart . . .

~AMY PENNINGTON BRUDNICKI

1

GRAN'S HOUSE

THINK OF A VESSEL THAT TAKES YOU BACK. WE ALL HAVE ONE. FOR SOME there's a song, others a fragrance, but for me, it's the memory of the house on the hill. Looking back, this was the place where time stood still. The mountains greeted me with cool serenity as if to wrap their arms around me and welcome me in. The rutted out driveway served as a compass leading me to where love was.

Granny and Grandpa lived in a white two-story house that was nestled in a clearing at the top of a hill in southeastern Kentucky. The front porch was long and narrow with two doors leading onto it, one from the living room and the other from a bedroom. There was a porch swing at the far end and many rocking chairs and rocking love seats lining the path to it. I was convinced that I could swing high enough to flip over the railing. That never actually happened, but mainly because there were always some set of "eyes" that kept me from doing that.

The porch had a ceiling that looked like a hardwood floor that you would see inside a house. When we sat on the porch in the evenings, we could hear the crickets and the frogs. It was peaceful there. This is where everyone rested after Granny's irresistible fried chicken supper and before the nail biting game of canasta for the adults or war for the kids. I liked playing war because so many of us could play at the same time. My cousins and I would sit in the middle of the living room floor and have four or five different decks of cards—all incomplete—I'm sure. The patterns were all very unique. Some of them were just plain ugly, but as long as they had Kings and Aces, no one cared. Sometimes we would play with buttons. Granny had a huge jar of buttons. The jar must have had peanut butter or pickled bologna in it at one time. Back then, in the seventies, both of these things came in enormous jars. The buttons were all different sizes and colors. There was one button that looked totally different than the rest because it had speckles all over it. We would scoop out piles of buttons for every player, and the one that ended up with the weird speckle button won. Looking back, it doesn't seem all that fun, but we sure liked the button game at the time.

I liked sitting in Granny's gooseneck rocking chair and watching as the little bird in the cuckoo clock made his appearance when the next hour had arrived. I liked the smell of the coal burning in the fireplace and the sounds of cards shuffling in the next room when the adults were playing cards.

Granny's house had many fireplaces that she used to heat her house with. She used coal and sometimes it would crack and spark when it was put in. They called it "spitting" and said that it meant that snow was coming. Granny had this black accordion-like fan thing for the fireplace. We liked playing with it, but she didn't like for us to. (Bellows is the correct term for the "accordion-like fan thing," in case y'all didn't know either.)

One of the bedrooms had a closed up fireplace. This was the bedroom that led to the porch. We liked to play in there, although there was something creepy about it. There was a picture on the wall. Maybe it was a painting. I can't clearly recall. It was of a man—my great, great grandfather—whose eyes seemed to follow you no matter where you were in the room.

Also in this room, there was an old time sewing machine, the type with an intricate iron design and a cast iron foot pedal. The foot pedal caused the needle to go up and down on the sewing machine. I guess people back then had nice looking clothes and nice looking legs because that was a workout. I know because I would "sew" from time to time. I used to pretend that I was driving a car and the foot pedal was my gas pedal. I would get it going real fast, but the bad thing about this idea was that my "car" got out of control occasionally. And by "occasionally," I mean every single time! My foot would slip off this cast iron bone crusher, and it would get trapped under this foot pedal, nearly breaking my little foot right off. I guess I was an optimistic kid because I would try it again and again. And, again and again, I would nearly die from pain, but I couldn't go cry about to anyone because no one was allowed to use the sewing machine except for Granny. Oh, the pain . . .

THE UPSTAIRS of Granny's house only had two bedrooms. The first bedroom had the stairs that came up into it with square "U" shaped banisters that looked down onto the stairwell. There were dormers in this room that you would split your brains out on. There were two queen size feather beds in this room and an old time radio with a round face and a dial that you could turn with a little post.

The back bedroom had two twin beds in it. The beds had lilac bedding on them, and I always thought it was neat that the beds always looked made when the pillow shams were on the beds. Also in this room was an old spinning wheel and tons of National Geographic magazines. I was always confused as to why these women would be photographed with their boobs showing. They should have called it "The Boobs Book."

Speaking of boobs books, my older cousins hid their girly magazines in a cavity in the floor. The recess was in the walkway between the two bedrooms and was covered by a floating wood plank. This had previously been a heat source from the dining room below. There was an opening so that the heat from the gas fireplace could rise and heat the upstairs. Anyway, once Granny discovered this filth hidden in the floor joist, the boys were out of luck. But they didn't need those magazines anyway when there were the yellow boob magazines in the back room!

Idle minds had to make their own fun in this day and time, and that's exactly what we created. In the front room, my cousin, Boose, and I were great humanitarians with our imaginary radio broadcasts. We were saving the world every chance we got. You see, in our fantasy, Dracula was on the loose. This was long before sparkly Edward Cullen changed the way we felt about vampires! Dracula, the evil vampire of the seventies, was on the loose, and we would warn the world. We would get on the radio—that's what we would say—and warn the world that Count Dracula was on the loose and headed right for them. Then we'd pretend that Dracula was at Granny's – upstairs at Granny's. Oh, the horror! I would run to the back room and hide in the closet with nothing but a little curtain protecting me. I really didn't know which was worse, having Dracula right outside the curtain or the brightly colored yellow boob digests at my feet. No one went down on our watch, and as far as I knew, Dracula never got near anyone thanks to Boose, me, and our radio broadcasting.

BACK DOWNSTAIRS . . . For some reason, I was convinced that the laundry area of the bathroom was haunted. It was dark, closed off by a curtain, and just scared me. It was little, but scary.

I ALWAYS LIKED Granny's dark little kitchen. It had enormous cabinets, they seemed nine feet tall. Roughly a dozen hooks lined the underside of the upper cabinets. They held hard plastic cup holders that you could insert disposable cups into. The cup handles hung from hooks much like a row of Christmas stockings would. They had the names of some of Granny's kids and in-laws on them: Haze, Meff, Mel, and many others. The pantry area had a refrigerator built in. I always thought that was neat. The door was flush with the kitchen wall with the remainder of the fridge sticking out into the pantry. Granny had a little plaque on the kitchen wall that said, "Kissing don't last; Cooking do." It had two cooks, kissing. It hung on the entranceway between the kitchen and the dining room.

Just outside the kitchen door, a round millstone served as a stepping stone to the back porch. The millstone was from the grist mill just across the creek. The stone itself was thick and round—like a giant concrete donut—with a two inch hole going straight down through the center. I always thought it was neat.

There was just something about being at Granny's. This was the place that everyone went to. It was peaceful there and chaotic at the same time with so many people. Granny had nine children, tons of grandchildren, and great grandchildren. In the summertime, they would come home for a week or two. Some of us lived in the holler near Granny, while others lived elsewhere in Kentucky. The rest lived in Alabama, California, Ohio, North Carolina, and other places too, I'm sure. When the visits were nearing an end, we would all line up and take pictures. This was usually a pretty difficult task. With so many little kids, they were always herding us like cattle to get us back in the picture.

THAT WAS the seventies and early eighties. And, oh what a time it was!

GRANNY AND GRANDPA are no longer with us. The house is still standing, nestled on the hill on Hurricane Creek. It's surrounded by quite a few more trees but much fewer people. As the house decays and deteriorates with age, it will always remain a vibrant memory in my mind that will never fade . . .

2

GOODIES

Several years ago at Christmastime, my niece, Natosha, made some delicious homemade goodies and delivered them in a colorful Santa tin.

A couple nights later, I woke up in the middle of the night and decided to have some peanut butter candy. It was even yummier at that hour since I was sneakin' a bite.

When I'd finished my samplin', I eased the lid back on, so as not to wake anyone, and turned quickly to get a drink. The worst scraping sound you ever heard echoed through the house. I turned back quickly to see what the noise was and made an even bigger racket when the tin crashed into the counter.

You see, in my quest to be quiet, I had accidentally closed the bottom of my shirt in the goody container.

Yeah ... not so stealthy!

3

THE BIRTHDAY CAKE

It was late November, my kindergarten year, and I was five years old. Mom made a gorgeous cake for my birthday celebration at school. It was a white rectangular shaped cake with little red candies dotted all over it. Mom sent this cake to school with us on the school bus. My brother was in charge of it and made sure that the cake made it to school without incident. After breakfast and before the bell rang to go to class, my friends and I were sitting around talking in the hall outside Ms. Howard's kindergarten classroom. I told them about this wonderful cake that Mom had prepared. They didn't want to wait to see it. And, being that I wanted to see it again myself, I devised a little plan that was about to go terribly awry.

I knew that my brother had made sure that my cake made it to the cafeteria in one piece and that the grumpy lunch ladies had stored it safely in the ginormous walk-in refrigerators. I also suspected that I could cook up a story that would cause them to release my beautiful cake into my custody. Well, I was correct. I don't recall my story, but I would bet it was chocked full of lies! Nevertheless, I was off to showcase my prize. I returned, and Boose, Lisa, and Susan all agreed that it was a gem of a cake.

As we admired it, someone else was noticing it, too. No, it wasn't my brother. It was this big kid who decided he was going to eat my cake. I'm sure he was just kidding, but you just don't tell a bunch of five-year-old girls something like that. We sprang into action and did the only thing that made sense at the time and the only thing that would assure the continued safety of my cake. We surrounded it . . . completely.

Someone went to get my brother when they saw what was happening. When he came down the hall, he couldn't believe his eyes! Not only was this cake that he had worked so hard to get to school *not* in the cafeteria, and not only was it amidst total chaos, it had also taken on a totally different form than the last time he saw it.

You see, the *only* way to keep my cake safe was to guard it. There were four of us, so we could protect all four sides. But *standing* guard is hard. So perhaps we squatted over the cake, you know, all of us back to back. But little legs wear out after a while. So, I suppose that the only sure-fire way to keep this big meanie from snatching my cake was to sit on it. And that's exactly what we did. We stood—uh—sat guard. My poor cake was smooshed beyond recognition! My brother nearly died. Come to think of it, *everyone* nearly died. My once beautifully decorated cake now resembled something that had been put through a printing press!

We didn't know what all the fuss was about. We protected the cake. We were still gonna eat it. But when Ms. Howard took the lid off the paper box, I realized what the ruckus was about. I no longer had a cake. I had a *pancake!* Later that day, my whole class still had cake, but I guess they had to spread it onto the plates with a spoon.

Can you imagine what laughter my cake evoked from the staff members who stole a peek at Mom's demolished masterpiece? I can say that Mom never sent a cake to school on the bus again . . . Come to think of it, I don't think she ever made a cake for school again, period! Hmmpt! Sit on a cake *one* time and they *never* get over it!

I can still remember Bub spilling the beans the second we got home from school, "*. . . and there they were, Mom. They were sitting on the cake!*"

4

THE EARTHQUAKE

November 5, 2014

HEARING about the earthquake felt in southeastern Kentucky today reminded me of another seismic event many years ago.

When I was a teenager, Mom and I were home alone one evening when all of a sudden the house started shaking. The mine down the road blasted all the time, so the house shaking was no new occurrence. You could always hear the hint of a blast beforehand, though. Then you'd feel the ripples as they moved across the land.

This day was different. As the earth began to shake, the only thing that could be heard was Mom bellering across the house, "Amy, I don't know what you're doing, but you're shaking the whole house!"

IT WAS AN EARTHQUAKE.

NOW, I've been blamed for a lot in my life, and I'll own up to most of it. But causing an earthquake ain't one of 'em!

5

THE RED HOTS

My cousin, Missy, and I were walking down Pound Mill one summer's day. We had just been to Sizemore's Market where we bought some red hots. I had a crush on the store owner's son, so I'd stop in often for the most random combination of things. Once, I bought a can of chicken noodle soup and a lemon. So, when I say I'd stop in for random things, I surely mean just that! The day I bought the lemon, he questioned the purchase. "A lemon?"

"We're using it to lighten our hair," I fired back. I should've used it to pucker my mouth shut, so I didn't say anything so stupid. But, that wasn't my forte'. It was the equivalent of Baby carrying a watermelon in Dirty Dancing. Only, in the end, she got Johnny. In my end, I got a cashier who thought I was crazy!

Anyway, back to THIS story . . .

Apparently, it wasn't bad enough to endure the summer heat *and* walking. No, we added cinnamon candy to the mix to balance out that trifecta of Hell! We were laughing, dodging vehicles, and trying to look pretty—you know the gist. All of a sudden, this dog came out of nowhere, snarling its lips, growling, and barking. Startled, I inhaled forcefully because it scared me to death. The force of that *inhale* lodged at least one red hot candy up the back of my mouth into my nose. It's something I just can't explain—searing heat cartwheeling toward your brain. I couldn't figure how to dislodge it, but Missy had a plan. To the best of her ability, she walked me through hocking a loogie. I don't even know if I'm saying or spelling that right. But, on that summer day, when we were trying to look pretty in case a handsome boy was close by, two "pretty" girls were hocking loogie's on Pound Mill Road.

OH, and that dog shied away REAL fast when its intended target started behaving like a demon possessed old man doing the hokey pokey in warp speed.

I'd never been judged by a dog before, but I'm fairly certain I was that day. It decided that my kind was nothing it wanted a piece or a part of. It tucked its tail and scurried away. I'm pretty sure it shot me the side eye as it retreated.

I don't know how you say, "Freak!" in dog, but, it said it. Twice.

AND THAT, my friends, is how I sucked a red hot up my nose. Backwards.

6

THE COSTUME PARTY

WHEN KIM AND I WERE LITTLE, WE DRESSED UP FOR A HALLOWEEN party at Rockhouse Baptist Church. In order to stay in character, we went the entire night without speaking to a soul; otherwise, our cover would've been blown. It paid off.

WE PLACED in the costume contest.

AT THE END of the evening, it was time to unveil the winners. We removed our floppy rubber masks so everyone could finally see who the little old woman and the little old man were. Yes, we dressed up as old people. Little old people. I was the freakin' man!

You've never seen cool until you've seen a ten-year-old *girl* dressed as a ninety-year-old man.

7

VACATION BIBLE SCHOOL

SOME OF MY BEST SUMMER MEMORIES ARE OF ATTENDING VACATION Bible School. Not only did we learn about Jesus, but we got to do a neat craft and activity every day. I remember one of those activities began with digging through a cardboard box of music makers. Every child would get an instrument or noise maker. We trekked all over the sanctuary of that little church with our drums, cymbals, maracas, rain sticks—just whatever we had access to. It was so much fun. I still remember marching down the aisle between the rows of pews and looking over at those stained glass windows; they seemed a hundred feet tall and so very beautiful!

I remember snack time, too. VBS always took place in temperatures that the Devil himself couldn't endure. And almost nobody had air-conditioning back then. Mercy, it was hot! We would line up and walk through the little snack building, as I called it, to get our snacks. They were always the same, year after year: a little styrofoam cup of Kool-Aid and two cookies on a napkin - one chocolate, one vanilla, both with cream centers. There was never enough drink because we were so hot from playing, but we were thankful for it just the same.

I'm not exactly sure what this building was used for, but I guess I could imagine it as a canning kitchen in days of old.

. . .

IF YOU NEEDED to use the bathroom, you had to use the outhouse on the hill. Outhouses always caused apprehension in me because, when I'd use them, I'd remember a story that my Aunt Daph told the first time we went to spend the night with her. She talked about baby chicks. For some reason, I thought they were inside the hole of the outhouse, and when I went to use it, I was afraid they'd bite me on the butt.

I'm sure I had that story *terribly* misconstrued. But I never made a trip to an outhouse in my entire life that I didn't think of that story!

MY MEMORIES of this church span beyond Vacation Bible School, too. I can remember going to Halloween parties at another structure on this property. I can't clearly recall it, but seems like it was a two-story old house with wood plank siding in the shade of chocolate brown. It sat just beyond what I called, "The Snack Building." Or maybe it was just the front side of the snack building. My memory tells me that there were three distinct structures, though. I need to make plans to revisit that hillside so that I can clearly recall some things.

Anyway, I can remember being inside a structure other than the church at a Halloween party. They had tons of fun activities to do. The one that stands out the most was apple bobbing. A bunch of us kids were circled around a metal washtub that was filled with water and apples. I remember plunging my face into the water and gnawing at an apple that the dozens before me had had a turn at. As I came up for air, I remember noticing the upstairs of this building. I made a mental note to slip off and explore when I was done annihilating an apple, but that opportunity never presented itself.

LOTS of wonderful memories were made on that hillside.

. . .

IF ANY OF you have ever stepped up to lead a whole slew of kids as a VBS leader, Halloween party coordinators, or Sunday school teachers, you have no idea the special memories these kids walked away with.

The memories I have of that little Presbyterian Church on the hill in Wooton, Kentucky, sure make me smile to this day.

8

SCARVES

I ENVY THOSE GIRLS WHO CAN WEAR SCARVES. I DON'T MEAN THE "scarves and mittens" scarf. No, I mean the "complement this outfit" scarf. My friends can do this effortlessly, especially my friend, Cassie.

I thought I'd give it a try. It's beautiful with its varying shades of maroon, the perfect hue for supporting my Leslie County Eagles or EKU Colonels.

THE PROBLEM IS, the scarf I bought could be a tablecloth - no kidding. I haven't sized it up, but I think it would fit my card table perfectly.

I'VE DONE THE TUTORIALS. I'm a bad girl. I either look like I have a giant plaid dinner napkin tied around my neck, or I look like I'm ready for the blizzard of '79!

IF YOU SEE ME OUT, and I have it tied around my neck like a cape, that's the look I was going for. We'll just say that my Superpower is persistence. I'll figure out how to wear it one way or another!

. . .

** UPDATE: I'm a liar. My superpower is lying. My beautiful dinner napkin/tablecloth/scarf is currently in a bag destined for the Salvation Army. I have to drive it around for a month or three, but it will eventually be donated. I couldn't figure it out. I'm a bad girl!

*** IT'S STILL BAGGED up in my bedroom floor. If the Salvation Army had a pick up service, that would suit me well!

**** IT'S NOT EVEN in the bag like I thought! I found it in my closet the other night. Lord have mercy. That thing is like a Ouija Board - you just can't get rid of it!

9

LEXIE

WHEN TYLER WAS IN PRESCHOOL, A YELLOW AND WHITE KITTY SHOWED up at the house. It didn't look puny or sickly, so I'd try to shoo it away. As determined as I was that she wasn't gonna stay here, she was equally as determined that she dang sure was.

Being a responsible human, I decided that I would print off some flyers and post them around the neighborhood—surely someone had lost their pet. Or wanted one.

SO, I TYPED UP A "FOUND" flyer and printed it off.

WHEN I REACHED to get it, there was nothing there. Thinking that I'd forgot to hit print, I did it again. Again, I reached for it. Nothing. The third time, I hit print and watched the printer, which was located on the bottom shelf of my computer desk where I was sitting.

THIS TIME, I discovered the problem. As the document printed, I saw a little hand ease forward, gently grasp the edge, and quietly retrieve it.

My sweet boy had taken them all. He didn't want someone else to have that cat. He wanted us to.

We sat him down and explained that we couldn't have a pet right then but that we'd find her a good home. He peeled those chocolate chip eyes up at us, with all the pleading that a little soul could have.

IT WORKED.

FIFTEEN YEARS LATER, she's still with us. She was here through elementary school, middle school, high school, and halfway through college.

I've decided that, when this world ends, all that will be left is Keith Richards, Betty White, and Lexie. Because none of them are ever gonna die.

1 0

MORE

IN A WORLD WHERE STATUS SEEMS TO BE DETERMINED BY THE THINGS WE have, what if we could adopt the old adage "Less is more?"

If you're safe and content with the life you have, it's ok to be satisfied with that.

Less really can be more. I don't need more kids, a bigger house, a newer car, another job, a bigger boat . . .

As PARENTS who only have one child, I can tell you that everyone has been quick to share their opinions with me about the behaviors of only children and how awful it is to raise one alone. I can promise you that very few people have reserved their opinions. What they don't know is that we have reasons for only having one child. That seems to matter very little to others, if they bother asking at all. I guess it's easier to drop an opinion and go on. I can say that our only child turned out to be a great kid. He's well liked, well adjusted, and was the valedictorian of his graduating class.

But what do I know? You know what they say about only kids . . .

Things may not have gone according to our plan, initially, but things worked out exactly as they should have.

. . .

EVER SEE a married couple who have no kids? I can guarantee the last thing they want to be asked is when they're having some. Imagine the number of times they've heard that. Did you ever stop to think that maybe they can't have kids? Now imagine how deep it hurts when they're questioned time and time again. Maybe it's not that at all. Maybe they just don't want kids, don't like kids . . . Why is *more* what they need? Maybe life has blessed them with a soulmate, fur babies, a passion driven job . . . It's not your place to assume that they need kids. Happiness doesn't hinge on having more.

UNDERSTAND that your definition of happiness isn't the baseline for someone else.

YOU BE YOU.

LET THEM BE THEM.

TRIP TO THE VET

BEING A RESPONSIBLE PET OWNER, THE FATEFUL DAY CAME WHEN BOTH the cat and the dog needed to go to the vet. Being that I didn't want to make *two* trips, I scheduled them both at the same time.

AFTER SOME WRESTLING, I finally stuffed the cat into her carrier. I learned the meaning of "cat fight" that day. And it's not that Willy Nilly hair pulling and love taps that boys describe. No, it's full on "claw your eyeballs out, don't let 'em take you down without a fight," claw to face, combat!

So, after the cat fight, I loaded the cat in the back seat and the dog in the front seat. The dog smelled like, well, she smelled like a wet dog. So, I had to roll the windows down. I threaded my hand through her leash and off we went on a short drive.

All went well until we arrived at the vet's office. I pulled into a spot right in front of the office, put the truck in park, then the dog jumped out the window. You can't make this stuff up! So, there I am, my arm half ripped out of the socket, and there the dog is, half hung. Well, that doesn't sound right, but you get the gist.

I unbuckle my seatbelt and scurry across the seat to free the dog. All is well and good until I get to the cat. She takes one look at the dog and then shats herself.

FOR THE LOVE OF PETE!

WE MAKE IT INSIDE, the technicians take the cat and clean her up before bringing her to me in the exam room. I have the blood scratched out of my face. I'm pretty much looking like Kramer from Seinfeld - disheveled and just sliding through life. And, I can *still* hear everyone laughing and asking about that dog that jumped out of the window!

I LEARNED some things that day: I can't multitask; the cat will never like the dog; dogs can fly; and, I'm not "man" enough to ever attempt a shared appointment at the Vet's office again!

1 2

THE SOUP KITCHEN

YEARS AGO, I PARTICIPATED IN A SOUP KITCHEN OF SORTS THAT RAISED money for a good cause. Bybee Pottery provided the bowls, and area community members provided the soup. It was a neat idea. We had to follow a recipe so all our soups were the same. Now, let me start by saying that I make a dang good vegetable beef soup. Dang good! I do when I use my recipe, that is. *This* soup called for Italian seasoning. I simply don't care for the flavor. It's horrid! Anyway, my soup was terrible. Just terrible. But, in my infinite wisdom, I figured that once my soup was mixed in with the others, it would all work out in the end. So, I loaded it up and headed to the church that was spear-heading this event.

I PULLED INTO THE LOT, expecting hoards of ladies to be piling in with steaming pots of goodness. There were two cars in the parking lot. Two. I said a silent prayer that what was happening wasn't actually what was happening, and I headed inside. Sure enough, those two cars belonged to the two people who were eagerly awaiting the first person to show up with their soup. I walked across the kitchen, the Imperial Death March echoing through my head . . . I handed my soup off—praying that someone—ANYONE, had got there before me. I heard every plop as my "Terrible, Horrible, No Good, Very Bad" veggie soup spilled out into a VERY empty industrial sized, stainless steel stock cooker. Number one. I was the First. One. There.

MY PLAN TO mingle my soup with the others had gone terribly wrong. I tore out of that parking lot with a valuable lesson that day: good things come to those who wait!

THE EARLY BIRD can keep the worm!

13

MAMMAW'S CORNBREAD DRESSING

THIS RECIPE WAS HANDED DOWN TO MOM FROM MAMMAW. IT'S Mammaw's signature cornbread dressing recipe—a recipe she created more than half a century ago. As is often the case with family recipes, the next cook in line changes it just a skosh. Mom put her spin on it, making minor adjustments, and handed it down to us.

This modified version is my take on it. Kim's may differ a tad. And yours will differ, still. That's ok.

DRESSING OR STUFFING, what do you call it? It's not worth your energy debating it. But I'll tell you why *we* call it dressing. Dressing is a side dish. Stuffing is something you shove inside a turkey or chicken! Call it what you will. The recipe is the same. As long as you're eating it, that's the only thing that truly matters.

SHOULD you have the desire to make your very own homemade dressing, here's the recipe:

. . .

INGREDIENTS:

Whole chicken

Chicken legs—about 10.

* Place chicken and 35 bouillon cubes, plus a stick of butter, in a pot.

(The more water you use, the more bouillon cubes you'll need. I can't tell you how much water I use, but the large stockpot I use holds a whole chicken and about ten chicken legs. I add water until those are well covered. I usually have about three quarts of broth in reserve after it's all assembled. Start off slow on the bouillon cubes, and add until it tastes right to you. For me, with all the water I use, that's a ton of bouillon cubes because I need enough broth to make two large pans of dressing. Again, add only a few. Once the chicken is fully cooked, and you can taste the broth, if it needs more flavor and sodium, add a couple more cubes. You can always add more, so definitely start out a little less heavy-handed.)

* Boil chicken until done. Once cooled, tear apart and loosely shred—not big chunks, but not stings, either. (I'm usually in a time crunch when I make dressing, so I wear rubber gloves like medical gloves to tear apart the chicken.) I'm very particular on which pieces of chicken make it into the dressing. Fat, gristle, joints—anything that wouldn't feel right in my mouth will never make it into my dressing. Some of you are laughing at this point. Some of you have never had a nasty chicken joint in your dressing. Gah! Ain't nobody got time for that nastiness!

You'll need three bowls when breaking down the chicken—the bowl with the cooled chicken, the bowl for the chicken that will actually make it into the dressing, and the scrap bowl. You're not done. Next, you're gonna go through the good chicken again as a precaution. I'm laid back about most things, but not this—absolutely no shortcuts. Don't make me whack you with a spoon.

Now that you're smiling, continue . . .

* DICE 4-5 STALKS OF CELERY, one large onion and a half of another.

Place in saucepan with some broth from the cooked chicken. Cook till softened.

* BAKE CORNBREAD. I use two large cast-iron skillets full.

- CRUMBLE CORNBREAD IN LARGE BOWL. Again, because I'm usually short on time, I wear gloves when crumbling the cornbread and shredding the chicken.

ADD these herbs and seasoning to the crumbled cornbread:
    - Add 3/4 jar RUBBED sage—not the short one.
    - 1 TBSP poultry seasoning
    - 1 box dry stovetop stuffing (you'll use this for the herbs). I get the chicken flavored one.

ONCE ALL THAT IS COMBINED, mix well, dispersing the seasoning throughout the crumbled cornbread. Then add the shredded chicken, onions, and celery. Once that is fully mixed, then start adding broth. Taste the mixture. If you think it needs more salt, add to broth then to dressing; It will disperse more evenly with that technique. Continue adding broth until the mixture is to the desired consistency. You don't want it soupy. But, if you don't add enough broth, your dressing will be too dry. It's a catch twenty-two that only playing with the recipe will teach you. I try to get it to the consistency that it would form a ball if I tried to shape it.

BAKE at 350° until it forms a crust. If you make it one night and bake the next day, you'll probably need to save some broth to spoon over it before you bake it. I always do. Save the extra broth, anyway. I freeze leftover broth and use it at a later time in homemade chicken noodle soup and chicken and dumplings.

YOU'LL DIRTY every dish in the house—twice—especially your big bowls; This, I can promise you. It's a labor of love but, man, is it yummy!

14

SANTA ON HURTS CREEK

WE WENT BACK to my hometown yesterday for a couple holiday celebrations - one, a late Thanksgiving, and the other was an early Christmas. In between events, we drove around to kill some time. As we started down Hurts Creek, I told my guys that when I was growing up, the house around the corner always had a giant Santa on the roof, and at night, they always had a spotlight on him. We rounded the curve as I pointed out the Brashear house.

THEN, I had a full on ELF moment. I screamed, "Santa! He's still there!" I was so happy, and they were pretty amused by my reaction.

THIS FAMILY HAS KEPT this tradition going for over fifty years now.

. . .

Santa on the roof will forever standout as one of my most favorite childhood memories.

15

CHRISTMASTIME IN MY HOMETOWN

I GREW UP ON HURRICANE CREEK, A HOLLER IN SOUTHEASTERN Kentucky. It was a truly special place. When I think of the true meaning of Christmas, this is where my mind, and most especially my heart, always travels to. Times were different then, simpler. It was the 1970s.

I remember our Christmas tree. The ornaments included little satin balls that were covered in tightly joined strands of thread, paper chains that we'd made at school, or colorful glass balls that were incredibly fragile. There were so many icicles cascading down the tree that they nearly eclipsed it. We had a little plastic Santa and his sleigh that we placed on our bay window ledge. Our decorations were simple but beautiful.

Mom would neatly wrap the gifts with ribbons and bows and carefully place them under the tree. The suspense was too much for little ones. Every year, it seemed, we'd call an emergency family meeting, my brother, sister, and I. The mission was always the same: somebody was gonna talk her down. We'd appoint a spokesperson, then the other two would wait. "Mom, please, please, pleeeaaassseee," we'd beg, "just let us open one present. We promise we won't ask to open annnny more. Pleeeaaassseee!" And, when she caved, we absolutely delighted in whatever we were given.

Christmas morning, when Santa came, we could always count on having an apple and an orange in our stockings. We got other things, too, but those two things were always in there.

We used to go Christmas caroling on Hurricane Creek. What an amazing memory! Lots of family lived around us - grandparents, aunts, uncles, and cousins. We'd bundle up then head out. Stopping by houses, we'd sing a variety of songs ranging from Silent Night to Rudolf. Often times, neighbors would invite us in to warm up by the fire. Sometimes they gave us hot chocolate and cookies. Other times, it was popcorn balls. Sometimes we simply got applause and the genuine smile of someone who appreciated our efforts. That was ok, too.

I can remember trudging up the road through the cold and the snow to take an elderly neighbor her Christmas gift. Her family had moved away, so we'd go visit her. Sometimes she'd send us down to the well to get fresh buckets of water. This was something she had difficulty doing, so, visiting neighbors always did it for her. I'm glad I was given that chore. It left me with a wonderful memory of a sweet little lady.

There was nothing better than snow days on Hurricane Creek. We were never short a playmate. Between siblings and cousins, we had a grand old time playing in the snow. We were either sleigh riding off the hill at Granny Maggards or Aunt Pats, throwing snowballs, or eating snow cream. Even if you were too cold to breathe, you weren't too cold to eat snow cream! It was the best.

My Christmas memories extend beyond the holler, too. On Hurts Creek, I remember a giant Santa on the Brashears' roof. I loved it. At night, Santa had a spotlight on him, so that was an extra special treat. I remember riding in the car and glancing up at that house. It was always so beautiful, but when Santa was up there, it was magical. I was awestruck. I know it couldn't have always been easy for them to carry on this tradition, but they'll never know what it meant to me and countless others that they did.

Traveling on into town, there was a store that had Mr. & Mrs. Santa displayed in the store window. They were electronic and had just enough movement to make my little imagination soar. I pretended they were real and could see me, too.

Closer to home, on Wendover, we always had Christmas plays up at the Big House, or the Garden House, to be specific. What a wonderful time in my life! We would perfectly depict the story of Jesus' birth. We had Mary, Joseph, wise men, and angels —all played by my siblings, cousins, neighbors, and friends. One year, we had the Jesus twins. Well, that wasn't part of the story, or the original plan, but during play practice, I kept stealing baby Jesus. I was three years old at the time, so any babydoll lying around seemed like fair game. The night of the play arrived, and they gave me a babydoll to hold so I wouldn't steal Him. Someone said I acted more like Judas than a sweet little angel. Nonetheless, it's still a precious memory to me. Sometimes the best stories are the ones that didn't go exactly as planned.

People often ask the place I'd most like to travel. After some consideration, I finally have an answer: Christmastime in my hometown, 1970 something . . .

VEGETABLE BEEF SOUP

- Stew beef - season to taste with seasoning salt, garlic powder, and pepper.
- Add diced onions (medium onion)
- Brown (I use medium/high heat.)
- I start browning mine in an old fashioned pressure cooker. I have an instant pot, but I've never used it for vegetable soup.
- After the onions and beef have browned, add five cans beef broth. Lock down lid and add weight. Turn burner to medium/high heat.
- Once it comes up to pressure, set timer for twenty minutes. This makes the meat extremely tender. Even the worst cuts of meat will be tender.
- Add a quart of home canned tomatoes. I mash them with a potato masher just enough to break them apart.
- Next, I transfer this to a crock pot along with the vegetables.
- 2 cans cut green beans
- 2 cans corn
- Celery & carrots

- Diced Potatoes

I MAY MAKE THIS HARDER THAN IT NEEDS TO BE. THAT'S OK. THIS IS THE recipe that I have perfected over the years, and that works well for me. I'm a firm believer in letting things simmer - Chili, Soup, Chicken & Dumplings, Soup Beans . . . You don't get the full flavor of anything if you don't give the ingredients time to mingle.

- Cook on high in crock pot about two hours.

17

BONUS PARENTS

Sometimes in life, someone comes along and steps into a readymade family. A package deal. In many cases, that role was created due to divorce. But, in our case, it was due to death. Our father passed away when we kids were very small.

If you are lucky enough to have someone who has filled this role, who was a good one, you need to thank them. Do you know how easy it would've been for them to walk away? Loving someone else's child isn't always easy. Heck, think of the times your own children drive you crazy. Sure, you love them. But, you have to; you made them. But, you don't always like them.

That stepparent *chose* to love them.

Our stepdad has had one of the most profound effects on our family. Not just our core family, but the whole family. He's one of the good ones. A truly good man. We're some of the lucky ones. To Clay, I want to say thank you for choosing us. We love you . . . so very much!

To my mother, brother, stepbrother, and sister, who are also stepparents, I want to say that I admire you all. You are all truly remarkable people.

I also want to say that we need to stop using the word "stepparent," and here's why. Think of a little stray puppy. If you take that dog in, make it one of your own, love it, and decide to keep it, it's no longer a stray. It's yours.

Clay, you're ours. You came into the mix and decided to claim us as your own. You're our dad, our Bonus Dad. How lucky we are to have had two.

APPRECIATE YOUR FAMILY, people, whoever makes it up. Love the ones who'll let ya. That's what I always say . . .

18

GLOW OF A BLANKET OF SNOW

FEBRUARY 2, 2018

I NOTICED something tonight that brought back a memory, a Hurricane Creek in the wintertime memory.

IT WAS THE 1990s. Mammaw and I had been down to Granny Maggard's house playing cards. Sometime around midnight, we decided to head home. We walked up the slick road, holding tight to each other so we wouldn't slip and fall—or, so we'd topple over together, I guess. Anyway, when we topped the hill, we stopped for a minute so Mammaw could rest. In that moment, I saw it. As I looked around, I saw a soft blanket of snow covering the hills and valleys of our little holler. And, from that fresh layer of snow came a glow; it perfectly illuminated every house and structure that dotted the winding road of Hurricane Creek. It was midnight, but yet, there was light.

. . .

MORE THAN TWENTY years have passed since that cold winter's night. Still to this day, when I see that glow, I remember that night.

AS I WAS GOING to bed tonight, I noticed the glow coming through the windows. It made me smile when my mind traveled back. And, for a moment, I was back on Hurricane Creek with my little Mammaw by my side.

19

LITTLE DICTATOR

My sister, Kim, is only one year and three days older than me. So, we were like twins—worse than twins, actually. Worse for me, that is, because Kim was a bossy little dictator who knew it all!

When I arrived on the scene, she thought I was cute. But after everyone went home, she realized that the new squirmy thing wasn't leaving, and she'd cry, "Bay ho." Which in baby speak meant, "Baby home." She wanted this new baby to go home. Kim didn't want me.

As a young child, she tried to flush me down the commode, and I was dumb enough to fall for this ploy. She pitched an irresistible plan. I was gonna see the Tidy Bowl Man! I wasn't too bright of a kid, but by the grace of God, I survived my infancy and toddler years. They say you block out traumatic things, so who knows what else she did to me. I was probably mailed to military school or the zoo at some point! I guess she realized I was here to stay, and then we began to have fun.

Mom had come up with an ingenious idea to keep us safe. She screened in the carport underneath the living room so us kids could ride our tricycles down there and play. Then she wouldn't have to worry about us getting in the creek or the road. It was a long carport, the same length as the house. There were screen doors on each end with hook and eye latches way up high where little hands could not free them.

One day we were riding our tricycles from one end of the porch to the other. Back and forth we'd go, and I guess the little prisoners in us hatched a plan — a devious, dangerous plan to escape. I don't recall whose idea it was originally, but we were both on the same wavelength. We, the Pennington Two, were busting out. We started our engines and revved the gas. Okay, we just rode as fast as we could until we did it. We busted out, literally. We busted right through the screen. We were free. We were lucky that our heads were still intact, but soon we would face the wrath of a mother who had spent money to keep her little angels, her little "Hell's Angels," safe. I imagine we didn't sit down on anything for quite awhile, if you know what I mean!

LIKE MOST LITTLE girls from our era, we had articles of handmade clothing and accessories — shawls, necklace change purses, hats, dresses . . . Our Aunt Sina made us blue jean purses for Christmas one year. Mine was a light denim color, in the shape of a half circle. It had a pocket on the front, the size of a regular blue jean pocket. "AMY," was stitched vertically down the shoulder strap in red thread.

Kim and I played many games growing up. One thing that we liked to play was "Mommies." I guess I was a lazy mommy because I always wanted to pack my babydoll in my blue jean purse. Well, my baby was longer than my purse, and she would always fall out. So, there my baby was, on the floor, and LD—little dictator—would spot her immediately. "You're gonna be a bad mommy!" she would say in her little high-pitched judgmental voice. Well, I was probably the one who inadvertently invented the ever so popular baby sling that lazy mommies everywhere are wild about! They're too lazy to carry their babies around, too!

You're welcome!

. . .

WE HAD A DETECTIVE AGENCY. Our agent names were "Lisa Lynn" and "Laura Lynn." I guess "Loretta Lynn" would have been the other investigator if we'd had another sister. I don't recall solving any crimes. I'm sure that "Lisa Lynn," aka, little dictator, aka, Kim, drove away all our business. I was the perfect child, being the baby and all, and Loretta didn't exist. So, it had to be Kim who ran our business into the ground!

Despite our failing detective agency, we had a booming business as chefs. Well, we only made one dollar while our bakery was in its prime, but that's more than we paid for supplies. So, that wasn't half bad! You see, we believed in keeping our expenditures low. We used only organic ingredients—another futuristic money maker. Our overhead was reasonable, as we worked from home, and the employees all worked for free. Come to think of it, I was an employee/part owner, so maybe that wasn't a good thing. But, for reasons unbeknownst to me, the Mud Pie Factory wasn't a great success.

We did know how to market the product, though. We knew when the coal miners got off work, and we would be waiting with our pies by the road. Actually, we were probably *in* the road.

One day, one generous miner purchased a pie. You know, come to think of it, I should sue him. I'm sure that some loony lawyer would take the case. Now, who was that coal dust faced man? If only I could remember! I could make millions because of emotional distress from thinking I could become rich. I could ask for pain and suffering because let me tell you, if you've ever received a grass blade cut, then you know how badly it hurts. And I had to have the grass because it was my secret ingredient. I could be a bazillionaire by now.

And, finally, we had the "Name Calling Game." Anytime we wanted to make Bub real good and mad, we knew what to do. All we had to do was call him a "big, fat (insert girl's name) lover." Looking back, we never actually knew if she was a real person or not, but for some reason, she got under his skin! We picked up on this fact and tormented him for years. I wonder if I called him up today and said that if he would remember?

· · ·

43

SISTERS DON'T ALWAYS GET ALONG. Kim and I shared a bedroom growing up. It was a fairly large bedroom with a cedar bedroom suite - twin beds, two chests, and a dresser. Or maybe one chest and two dressers. I never could get the names of those straight. We had two tall ones and one long one, got it? My bed was on the left, and Kim's bed was on the right with the tall one between the beds underneath the window. At the foot of Kim's bed, before you reached the closet, was the long one. At the foot of my bed, before you reached the door, was the other tall one.

Ok, as I previously stated, sisters don't always get along. Kim and I would get mad at each other, and the fight was on. We would divide the room with black electrical tape, from the ceiling to the floor. One of us, the one who was the maddest, would climb on the tall piece of furniture between the beds and run a line of tape from the ceiling, all the way down the wall to the floor and across — all the way out the door to the hallway.

In order for me to go on Kim's side, I had to pay her one penny. And, in order for her to come on my side, she had to pay me one penny. If I wanted clothes or toys out of the closet, I had to pay Kim. And if she wanted to use the bathroom, or eat, or just not look at me anymore, she had to trespass on my side and had to pay me one penny.

Now, one would think that I, the owner of the door, would be rich. And, that she, the owner of the clothes, would be rich. But there was a slight problem. There was a thief among us. We would steal our money back when the other one went out of the room. I'd steal from her, she'd steal from me . . . Days would pass and then we'd finally tear the toll tape down and get along for a while longer. Oh, I said that the Lynn Detective Agency didn't solve any cases. But that wasn't true. We realized that we were each stealing from the other, so I guess that is a case solved.

As I GOT OLDER, I was part of a band. No, I'm not referring to my stint in the Hyden Elementary band where I played the ever so beautiful clarinet. I must have played very well because people would tell me to stop playing. This could *only* mean that I was so amazingly talented that I didn't even need to practice, or possibly even waste my musical giftedness or time by showing up for concerts.

No, the band that I'm referring to was my Bon Jovi gig. I had a cushy stage, many unique microphones, and the stage lighting was phenomenal! We celebs are so lucky to have all these perks. I didn't want to take away from the boys in the band with my outrageous ability, so I would usually perform solo. Sometimes Boose, Jeannie, or Nicole would perform with me.

Our stage was the afore mentioned cedar twin beds. They were spaced perfectly so that I could jump back and forth across them. It's important to be an energetic performer. My mic was any hairbrush that I could get my hands on, and the stage lighting just so happened to double as a makeup mirror. I feel, and always have felt, that it's important to improvise. My sound crew was Boom and Box. I still perform with Jon and the boys today. And, just like days of ole, they have no idea . . .

20

HURRICANE CREEK MINE DISASTER

THIS STORY IS NOT FROM MY OWN MEMORY BANK, BUT RATHER MY account of a mine disaster that happened just down the road from where I grew up.

DECEMBER 30TH, 1970, began as any other day in the coalfields of southeastern Kentucky. On this morning, a group of hardworking miners started their day before the sun came up. They'd never see another sunrise. Shortly after noon, disaster struck when the Finley Coal Mine - located on Hurricane Creek in Hyden, Kentucky - exploded, killing all thirty-eight men inside.

The lone survivor, A.T. Collins, was about to enter the mine when the explosion occurred. The blast pelted him with debris, ripping his clothing and tearing the watch from his wrist. Lucky to be alive, he was left battered and bruised—blown some sixty feet from the mine's entrance.

IN THE SEVENTIES, when the disaster occurred, all homes on Hurricane Creek that had phone service were on a party line —one phone line shared by many households. My aunt, who was visiting from Alabama, was on the phone with her husband when the officials from the mine came on the phone stating that they needed her to clear the line, that the mine had blown up.

I can only imagine the chill that she experienced when she heard those words because I know she felt the explosion shake the house. My Granny's house, where she was visiting, was just around the bend from the mines.

THIRTY-EIGHT MEN WENT underground that fateful day, miners who labored hard, day in and day out, for the families they loved. As darkness fell, those men—the husbands, fathers, grandfathers, uncles, sons, brothers, friends, and neighbors—didn't return home.

Lives were forever changed. Routines were forever changed. And hearts were forever broken. The wife who watched every day as her husband approached the door with coal dust covering his face and a lunch bucket in his hand, she had become a widow. The children who waited for Daddy to tuck them in at night, their world had fallen apart. And the mother who had to bury her son- I can't even imagine her pain. In the blink of an eye, devastation struck these families . . . and the effects are still felt to this day.

IN 2011, a memorial was completed on Hurricane Creek in honor of the thirty-eight men who lost their lives on December 30th, 1970. They are the true unsung heroes of Appalachia.

Today, more than forty years later, these men live on in the hearts of their loved ones. Gone, but not forgotten . . .

21

GRANDPA PENNINGTON

WHEN I WAS AROUND SIX YEARS OLD, MY GRANDPA PENNINGTON called one day. I answered the phone. He asked what I was doing. I told him that I had gone to the refrigerator looking for carrots and celery, but we didn't have any.

A little over two hours later, we did. My grandpa drove straight to our house from Berea, a two-hour trip. We certainly had other food in the house to eat. But he knew I wanted something I didn't have. He remedied that.

I REMEMBER BEING at the Drugstore once with Grandpa. We were sitting on the barstools at the counter. He handed me a dollar and told me to split it with my sister. I was very young. So, I did exactly that.

I hopped down off the barstool, found Kim by the gumball machines, and ripped that dollar right in half.

I can't say that Grandpa was proud of my barbaric technique. But I'm quite certain he was amused. I'm guessing he got a big kick out of retelling that story for many years to come.

· · ·

My Grandpa Pennington was a good man who loved us so. I'll never forget the love in his eyes when he looked at us. In any picture that I recall seeing of us and Grandpa, he was never looking at the camera. He was always looking at us. Always.

Daddy had passed away at that point. I'm sure seeing us was like looking at extensions of Daddy. Grandpa poured all the love he had for his child and his grandchildren into one glance when he looked at us.

It's been nearly forty years since I last saw my grandpa. Still yet, I remember the unconditional love he had for us.

22

LEARNING TO DRIVE

I'M NOT SURE HOW OLD I WAS WHEN I FIRST BEGAN LEARNING TO DRIVE. I do know that Mom insisted that us kids learn to drive a stick shift. Her exact words were, "You'll never find yourself in a situation you can't get out of." Pretty good advice.

Driving wasn't exactly second nature to me, so the only soul who was brave enough to help me learn was my brother. The problem with a fearless brother teaching you to drive was that he made you do things that weren't safe—or legal—like doing a U-turn in the middle of the Hyden Spur. Without warning. Like a little driving dictator!

I'd like to say that I felt like Mario Andretti on those days. I got up to speed, started into my turn, and drifted like a boss until I spun back the direction we just came – wind whipping through my hair, southern rock spilling through my speakers, head nodding along to that sweet soulful sound. Looking cool. Being cool.

Yeah, I'd like to say that, but every word of it would be a lie. It was more like gripping the steering wheel until I was certain my knuckles would crack trough my skin, sweating like I'd just ran a marathon, neck whipping back and forth from the engine dying—lurching the car forward like it was hiccupping—never being completely at ease because I knew the "turn" command was coming any second.

Even though I didn't do it well, I did do it, and we somehow survived those scary driving days. Those long, dark, dreadful days. And then came time to get my license . . .

23

DRIVER'S LICENSE

I REMEMBER CLEARLY WHAT I WORE THE DAY I GOT MY DRIVER'S LICENSE —a pair of dressy shorts with a matching black and white checkered blazer jacket. I wore my hair in a French braid with my big eighties bangs standing tall. I felt so sophisticated. I have no idea how or why I remember this, but it's etched in my memory. I don't know if it was sunny, cold, rainy—nothing. I just remember my clothing. Priorities.

So, after more practice than any one human should need, the day had come when I finally had the courage to try for my license. Being that I didn't want to give myself, nor the instructor whiplash by driving our stick shift, I opted to borrow Mammaw's car for the driving test. Her car was a *sporty* little automatic station wagon with fake wood grain on the sides. I was pretty much the envy of all in attendance.

Before we left for the test, I told my sister that the only thing that concerned me was parallel parking. I was afraid that someone would drive too closely behind me, and I wouldn't be able to do it. I was scared, she was available, and just like that, a plan was born.

The parallel parking portion of the test came. I looked in my rearview mirror and knew that things were progressing as they should. What I saw when I looked in the mirror was my sister in her vehicle, *way* back behind me, blocking traffic. With a sigh of relief, I gave it a whirl and am happy to say that I completed that dreaded task successfully on the first try. I passed the remainder of the test with flying colors, as well, and was granted an affirmative smile by the instructor lady before she handed over my card stating that I had met the requirements of the Commonwealth of Kentucky and had finally become a licensed driver.

I headed back inside the courthouse where my friend, Diana's, mom took the picture for my license.

I ALWAYS SAY that I'm like Rain man with the random things I remember - French braid, checkered suit, and Mrs. Joann taking my picture. When I think about it, I guess I recalled all I really needed to know about that day.

2 4

THE WEDDING OF THE CENTURY

I FINALLY FOUND A BOYFRIEND WHO EVERYONE LIKED, ME INCLUDED. HE was respectable, had a good job, and was incredibly funny. *Now where's my club? I can't let this one get away!*

Bru and I met in February 1995. By May, we were engaged-without the use of the previously mentioned club, threats, or Clay's guns! We planned an April 1996 wedding. I had Bride magazines galore, was getting invitation samples mailed to me, and had been trying on wedding dresses. We were going to have the wedding that little girls dreamed of! Not me, though. I was a tomboy and thought boys were stupid. I had plans to live with my Mommy forever. Soooo, it's a good thing I really didn't have any heartfelt dreams about the perfect wedding. Nevertheless, I was in planning mode! It didn't take much planning to realize that our *wants* were more than our *budget* could afford. We decided to scale back on the expenses, but to push forward with the wedding–as in, December 1995. And no, I wasn't pregnant!

I heard about a girl from my hometown who had gone to Gatlin-burg, Tennessee, to get married. They talked of how beautiful the wedding pictures were, the perfect little chapel, and how she had saved a ton of money. So, loving the best of both worlds, I approached

Bru with the idea. He thought it was a good idea, too, so I began contacting chapels in the Gatlinburg, Tennessee, area. It was going to be perfect!

One of the places that we did not contact was the Chapel of Love. I pictured a drive through wedding ceremony. That was the cheesiest sounding place. Vegas is all I could picture in my mind. So, they were out of the running. We contacted lots of places. Who knew they would have so many chapels in a tourist area?

One that ranked high on my list was the Chapel in the Village. I could just imagine the beautiful chapel nestled in a quaint little town and a meadow gently flowing nearby. They even put a "love" stamp on the envelope when they responded to our inquiry. That was a small thing, but they obviously had an eye for detail.

After much thought-not really. I wanted the chapel, the meadow, the quaint town . . . So we chose the Chapel in the Village.

It was November when we settled on a location for this fairytale wedding. Bru and I were flying down to Florida for Christmas that year and would be there for two weeks. Our time was quickly fading to go see the perfect place before the big day. As it turned out, all those weeks came down to one weekend that we could fit in a trip to Tennessee before our Florida trip. We got up on a Saturday morning, planning to head south, but were greeted by a big snow. This meant that the place where we planned to wed would remain sight unseen until the big day. That was ok, though, because we felt like we already had been there. As a matter of fact, I could imagine the gentle flow of the water as it strolled down its banks . . .

I called the wedding coordinator many times to work out details. I was sad that only fifteen people could come. I guess the chapel was smaller than I first thought. Nevertheless, this wedding was going to be amazing because we were saving so much money. She informed me they had dresses. "Wedding dresses?" I asked enthusiastically.

"Yes," she responded.

When I asked her to describe them, she told me they had many styles to choose from. Never having been to Gatlinburg, or anywhere, really, I had no idea what this next sentence meant. She said they tied in the back. Hmm . . . tied in the back? That sounded odd, but they were wedding dresses, after all. So, I was still sure that that was ok. I was certain you must not be able to tell. They had outfits for Bru to choose from, too. So, this was shaping up quite nicely!

All was in order, and we flew down to Florida. I was to meet Bru's dad for the first time. So, I was a little nervous about that. Wanting to make a good first impression on him, I dressed very nice. I wore a black, velvety dress and heels. Ok, what moron does this? I had to go through an airport dressed like a madam, and my feet were screaming. I really did like this dress and actually had plans to wear it out to dinner the night of our wedding. No reception for us, we were just gonna have a nice dinner.

Bru's dad didn't like the idea of us sleeping in the same room before we were married. His mom convinced him that it would be fine because of the twin beds' sleeping arrangements. I don't think he loved the idea, but he accepted it.

The day came for us to leave Florida. My soon-to-be in-laws gave us a car, and we headed back to Tennessee for the Wedding of the Century . . .

When we arrived in Gatlinburg, we checked into our honeymoon suite and set off to find a place to do my hair. I was wearing a tracksuit, and she asked me to take my tee shirt off so that I didn't ruin my hair when I changed clothes. No one could tell that I didn't have a shirt on underneath the jacket, so that was ok. The lady's name was Amy, and she gave me two pieces of advice. She said I was too young to be getting married. And that I was too young for gray hair. I informed her that I was twenty-three. And what did she mean, I had gray hairs? I think her eyeballs were fogged over by the cigarette smoke in the room. There was some sleazy man talking to Amy, the stylist, who was smoking up a storm. She was really into talking to him and not paying much attention to the spray glue that she was applying to my head. I don't think a Mac truck could have given my tresses a tousle!

. . .

WHEN MY HAIR WAS FINISHED, Bru and I went back to the room where I re-did some of my hair that looked odd. It was time to emerge, so we headed off the hill into town. We had a hard time finding the chapel, but finally matched up the address with a building.

With its shop-like appearance, it didn't look much like a church, but we went inside anyway. You know how when you step inside a chapel you see the two long rows of pews, the pulpit, beautiful flower arrangements . . . Everyone knows what a chapel looks like. But apparently, I was *badly* mistaken because *my* chapel looked nothing like that. *At all.* I knew the rows of pews would be small since only fifteen people could attend, but they were *so* small, in fact, I couldn't even see them. I couldn't see a pulpit either! All I saw was the shyster who was masquerading as a preacher! There was nothing even remotely resembling a chapel in the "chapel." I felt like I had just stepped into my worst nightmare! I had people coming to see me get married, and there was no chapel!

Even though this place was not exactly what I had planned on, I loved Bru, and there was no reason why I should not get married on this day.

Once I was over the architectural shock, it was time to move on to full-blown *heart attack* mode! You see, I was about to see my beautiful wedding dress for the first time. The daughter of Reverend Shyster came to me so I could select my wedding attire. This was my wedding coordinator, and I wondered how she would coordinate her black eye and fat lip when I was done with her. Anyway, have you ever wanted to crawl under a rock and *die*? Well, I was looking for my rock when she held dresses up, side by side, and asked, "Do you want to be the Saloon Girl or the Southern Belle?" (This is a wholesome book, so I just had to backspace some words out of this story . . .) Words cannot describe the non-southern hospitality that I wanted to open up on her at that very moment! The shock that I felt shook me to the core. For my chapel in the village, nestled in a quaint little town with a meadow gently flowing nearby, was no chapel at all . . . It was an old time photography studio. Holy cow! What had I gotten myself into? As much as I needed a doctor on hand to ward off the heart attacks that I was *sure* were coming, Bru and I both decided that we were getting married here at the Shysters of the Village that was crammed into a tourist town with no pews, no pulpit, no freakin' meadow, and *no real wedding dresses!*

So my wedding attire options had suddenly diminished, and I was left with wearing the tracksuit that I currently had on or the black, velvety dress that I had brought along to change into to wear to our nice dinner afterward. Being that I didn't want to be *too* casual, I opted for the black dress. It's not very traditional, I know, but it fit this fiasco just fine!

It was time to get changed into my "gown." Being that I was wearing fake fingernails and couldn't do anything with them, my sister, Kim, had to assist. They showed us to the changing room, which was a closet at best. So there we were trying to get pantyhose on me in a closet. It was a hard task, but Kim finally got those things on me! If you ever want to know how easy that was, just tie rubber bands around your legs and try to do the hokey pokey!

Bru and I were finally dressed. He in the outfit he had planned to wear to dinner after the "ceremony" and me in my Elvira outfit! We proceeded upstairs in this dress shop of horrors. There was still hope, I thought. Maybe the pews, pulpit, and a freakin' *miracle* were up there!

Uh . . . NO! It was even smaller than the downstairs. When I reached that top step and looked to the right, I was greeted with a selection of ratty looking bouquets, maybe a dozen of them. The walls were covered with dark paneling. There was a double window that I wanted to jump out of. The space might've been eight feet wide and four feet deep. You might think there's more to this description of the "sanctuary." Sadly, you're mistaken.

All those who showed up for our wedding couldn't even fit. Kim, the maid of honor, and Clay, the best man, crammed in there with us. She was wearing a beautiful ivory lace dress and Clay was wearing a suit. So when the preacher got upstairs, he thought that *they* were the ones getting married.

Bru and I stood with our backs to the window, Reverend Shyster in front of us, and the ratty bouquet selection to our right. Everyone else had to stand in the stairway.

We finally said our "I do's." Then, preacher man morphed back into shyster man and tried to sell us everything for something ninety-five. He tried to sell me a picture of me writing my married name for the first time for nineteen dollars and ninety-five cents. He even tried to sell us a cake that the couple before didn't pick up because they didn't get married. Guess it snowed the day they were gonna check out the shysters, too! I was already mad as could be that our story-book wedding was more like a page out of Ripley's Believe it or Not, so we declined. But my Uncle Tony thought that ours was the funniest wedding he had *ever* been to. So he bought it!

When the wedding was over, Bru's Uncle Pete, who had come in from Chicago, asked him how many times I'd been married! I guess he'd never seen a bride wear a black dress to a wedding before! Well, guess what, Pal? Neither had I!

As we were leaving the "chapel," my cousin, Lori, and her husband had just shown up. We literally opened the door to leave and there they were. She said, "I have jewelry." I appreciated the offer, but what I needed was vodka! Not that I even drank, but this was a *fine* time to start!

Someone recommended a restaurant. As we were looking for it, we passed a beautiful white chapel that was nestled back away from the road. I thought how perfect it would have been and that's when I saw its name, "The Chapel of Love."

A few months after Bru and I were married, we were watching America's Most Wanted. I kept thinking, "Who does that little shyster guy remind me of?" I looked over at our wedding picture of Bru, me, and Reverend Shyster. Then it hit me. The guy who married us was on America's Most Wanted. I couldn't believe it. Well, actually, I could! There was no mystery that that guy wasn't exactly on the up and up.

Bru and I called them and gave our story. He sure didn't want to, but I can be a persuasive gal when I'm fired up about something. The guy from America's Most Wanted said, "Let me get this straight. You think you married the guy?" I guess he thought we'd *both* married the guy!

I can understand the confusion.

I clarified, "No! He married us. As in, he was our preacher."

Turns out, he wasn't the same shyster guy. But it sure wouldn't have surprised me! The way we knew *our* guy and *that* guy wasn't the *same guy* was because our Reverend wasn't as tall as the guy they were looking for. Nevertheless, he was as crooked as the day is long, and I wouldn't be surprised to see him on there one day!

MOST PEOPLE HAVE wonderful memories of their wedding day with beautiful photos to remind them of the best day of their lives. But you know what? Those make for humdrum stories. We can laugh about it now, and people never seem to tire of our story of the Wedding of the Century.

25

BOOSE

SOMETIMES IN LIFE, YOU COME ACROSS A TRULY SPECIAL PERSON WHO has a profound impact on your life. For me, that person is my cousin, Boose.

We were born in 1972. Being that we were family, and the same age, we were instant BFFs. We were in the same grade in school, so that lent to many shenanigans over the years.

In the 1970s, we wore matching Betty Boop shirts—the type that had colorful prints and was made out of unbreathable polyester. They were absolutely horrid and hot on scorching summer days, but all the girls on Hurricane Creek had them.

Boose taught me how to ride a bike. Then, I nearly killed her when I caused us to wreck on hers. That was bad times!

ON INTO THE 1980s, we roamed Hurricane Creek. We were from one end to the other visiting a horse named Star, traipsing down to the mines, or even walking up to the highway where we went to Jeff Mart for a candy bar and cold pop. All the while, Mom thought I was at Boose's, and Aunt Helen thought she was at my house.

One time when we were bebopping around the holler, we decided to sit on Uncle Elb's bridge. We dangled our feet over the edge and sat there and talked.

As the conversation continued, we spotted a honeycomb in the creek. I don't know what came over us, but the next thing I knew, we were down there fishing it out of the water. We brought it back to the bridge and sat there and ate it! It was *obviously* in the creek for a reason. We had food at home—honey, even—so I don't know why we thought we needed *that* honey. *But* we lived to tell about it, so it all worked out.

WHEN WE WERE in sixth grade, we entered ourselves into a competition. We signed up before we had our talent lined out—maybe not the smartest move.

We finally settled on drawing. The only problem was that I couldn't draw. At all. She could.

The day of the competition arrived, and I still couldn't draw. All her teaching had been for naught because this old girl still drew with all the skill of a six month old baby.

Having no other option—and fessin' up wasn't an option—we did the only thing we could. Before we went to the program, she lightly sketched the outline of a horse. Yes, we were the Milli Vanilli of the art world before Milli Vanilli was a thing!

Anyway, we got to the venue—I'm pretty sure it was a church. When it was our turn to present, I talked while she drew, then we switched spots. As she talked, I Picasso'd my way through it as if I were an old pro!

We didn't win. But we didn't get caught, either. So, that's basically *still* a win.

THAT SAME YEAR, a radio station came to town. We were *all* about the music, listening every day. Then they opened a request line. Being that we were notorious prank callers, we were all about *that,* too!

As if it were our civic duty, we'd call every day. Only, we had lots of requests—and they got a little bent out of shape if you called too often.

Soooooo, we did the only thing we could do. We called back to back to back . . .using disguises. Sometimes we had women's voices, sometimes men's. We'd use a sexy voice then a big burly one. We'd pretend to be a child. Or a foreigner. That opened a whole other slot for our impersonations.

That ole request line didn't stay open more than a year or two. And I can think of two specific reasons why that was—Audrey and Amy!

My apologies, citizens of Hyden.

TIME PASSED, and we were now in the seventh or eighth grade. We were in Mrs. Crawford's homeroom. Boose found a three-legged chair one day in the trash section of the third floor hallway. She thought it would make a nice addition to the classroom, so she ushered it right in.

It was wrong, but we'd delight in exchanging classmates chairs with that jalopy. It provided hours of fun! That's an exaggeration, but we had a big time.

Anytime we'd spot the chair tossed out in the junk pile, we'd haul it back in. I'm not sure how no one ever saw us lugging a three-legged chair up three flights of stairs—repeatedly—but they didn't.

Mrs. Crawford was always flabbergasted as to how that chair had made its way back into the classroom. I'm sure she had some bad kids she suspected as the culprits. But I don't think she ever suspected Boose, Twynell, Rachel, or me. And it was us. Every. Single. Time!

IT USED to be a big thing to sneak into high school dances as eighth graders. Well, I don't know if it was a thing, but it was a big deal to Boose and me that they thought we looked old enough to be there.

Anyway, Boose and I were sitting on the floor waiting for the next song to come on. We didn't have dates to this forbidden dance, and a slow song had just come on.

This guy comes up to me and asks me to dance. Mind you, I had my back to him, so I didn't see him.

Boose said, "Dance with him, Aim. He's cute!"

That's all I needed to hear. I was up on my feet and on him like an octopus. It was in that moment that I got a good look at him, and so did Boose.

She was somewhat mistaken in her hasty assessment of his cuteness.

As he and I danced, I'd shoot daggers at her every time he spun me around in her direction.

This fella squeezed my guts out and smelled like he worked in the Marlboro cigarette testing line.

It was the longest song of my entire life. "I Can't Fight This Feeling Any Longer," by REO Speedwagon wasn't *speedy* at all. In fact, it felt like it lasted forty-seven years. If not forty-eight.

THE HIGH SCHOOL years were now upon us. Boose's artistic abilities were now being recognized by the art teacher at LCHS. Boose was asked to paint a mural above the lockers in the hallway. It always made me proud to pass that section of the hallway because my boo's talent was front and center for the whole school to see.

Boose and I both took Home Economics, or "Home Ec" for short. Unfortunately, we were placed in different classes. While she won the Home Ec award for her class, I didn't exactly excel.

Sewing wasn't second nature to me. Mrs. Hendrix came at me with that seam ripper more times than I care to count.

I loved her, though, and so did Boose.

ANOTHER TIME IN HIGH SCHOOL—AND I'm not saying *when*—we had a project due where we had to cite our source. Boose and I were in different classes and each started this project the night before it was due.

We drove to Chad Morgan's house in the snow and borrowed a book for the paper. It was great, providing us with lots of information.

But, in order to make our projects longer, we had to embellish some things. That came in the way of us making up a fictitious book. The title, author, publishing company, passages, and page numbers—they all were fictitious!

Somehow, we didn't get caught.

IN A WAY, that book creating was a prelude of things to come. As it turns out, we both went on to become writers. Only, we're on the up and up these days when we create books.

SPEAKING OF THESE DAYS, we also went on to become singers. Well, Boose actually can sing and has the guts to do it.

I'm more of a slapstick singer who just wants to have fun slaughtering lyrics. I'm the queen of misheard lyrics. When I belt out all the wrong words during our Cousin Karaoke segments on Facebook, my partner in crime just rolls with it.

We think we're highly entertaining, and tens of fans would agree.

I'm not sure what Miss Bass, our high school chorus teacher, would say about our antics, though. Can you still get detention in your forties? Asking for a friend . . .

ONCE OUR HIGH school days were over, I tried to kill us once again when the car I was driving was T-Boned.

Memory tells me there was yet another car wreck, but for the life of me, I can't recall it.

All these antics earned us a lifelong ban on being in the same car together. I'm sure Cousin Karaoke strikes fear in our people for more than one reason—the singing and the fact that our studio is our cars.

. . .

I SAID all that to say this. Boose is my person, and I love her. We've shared a lifetime of memories together. She's funny, smart, empathetic, and so very strong. In times of trouble or heartache, she's like a lighthouse in stormy seas; everyone can see the storm around her, but they also see her unwavering strength. She's such an inspiration.

I reckon I'm her person, too. We've been each other's shelter in the storm more times than I can count. She hears me when I'm silent. Not everyone has a friend like that. It takes a special person to hear what isn't being said.

Boo, when you read this, just know that I love you awful and couldn't write a book of my little stories without including a special chapter just for you!

I haven't even begun to scratch the surface on all the shenanigans we've lived through or the memories we shared. But I'll bring this literary chapter to a close.

Lucky for us, our story is still being written, so our chapter will never come to a close . . .

26

PLANTING MEMORIES

I REMEMBER THE HILLSIDE BETWEEN THE CREEK AND GRANNY Maggard's house when I was a little girl. On those first warm spring days, when winter faded away, the slope was painted yellow with a multitude of Easter flowers that had emerged. It was the prettiest sight to behold. Their proper name is daffodils. To me, they will always be Easter flowers.

Years later, after I was married, Bru and I went back home in the spring of the year. Our main purpose for the trip was to go to Granny's house so I could pick flowers.

The white two-story home had long been vacant by this time. It lived a lonely existence now in that clearing. Laughter no longer rang out on that hillside and cousins no longer stampeded through the mountains while their parents sat on the porch visiting. Still yet, as we walked up the hill, the Easter flowers were there to greet me, as if nothing had ever changed. Just like that, I was a little girl again glancing at the most beautiful sight I'd ever seen.

"Picking flowers" became *digging* flowers. We found a spoon, and that served as our shovel. A very short shovel. A few sprout bundles into the endeavor, we had busted up knuckles. Then it started to rain. We were a muddy mess by the time we left Hurricane Creek, but it was worth it because I had done more than picked flowers that day. I was about to transplant memories.

Now, every year, as winter fades away, my treasures from Hurricane Creek begin to emerge. They signify that spring is here. But, they do more than that. They serve as reminders of a wonderful time in my life when Mammaw and Granny were still with us, when cousins were plentiful and present on a daily basis, and when a little house in the mountains of southeastern Kentucky was full of love and life.

Sometimes we have to be deliberate in our recollections and purposely put things in our path that give us happiness. If you're lucky enough to still have your parents or grandparents with you, I suggest you do the same as I did. Transplant a memory if you can. Your knuckles will heal, and the mud will wash away. But, when you plant a memory, it's there forever.

AND, forever just might be long enough . . .

27

MOM

MY PARENTS WERE THE QUINTESSENTIAL HIGH SCHOOL SWEETHEARTS who fell in love and got married. Mom was just shy of her senior year.

Suddenly, Mom—the Beatles loving teen, who had once professed she'd be a Saloon Girl one day, one day long before she knew what that *actually* meant—had become a new bride and a new mother when my brother was born.

THE LITTLE FAMILY would move around from town to town so Daddy could find work. They'd lived in several areas in Kentucky and Ohio when they finally moved back home to Hyden.

MY SISTER WAS BORN; and then I was. It was now the early seventies.

ONE DAY, Daddy kissed us all and left for work. Mom said he came back in and kissed us all again.

You see, the brakes on his coal truck were bad. The company told him he could work, or they'd find someone to replace him. Being a man of honor and duty, and having a family to support, he went to work.

Later that day, a state trooper came to the door and delivered the devastating news that Daddy had been killed in a coal truck wreck. He was twenty-four years old.

MOM WAS TWENTY-THREE.

WHILE SHE HAD the family to lean on—both hers and his—the road ahead was a scary one and so very uncertain.

SOMEHOW, she forged on. She got her GED, and once all us kids were in school, she went back to school herself. Attaining a goal she set as a small child when she had been inspired by the work of Mary Breckinridge—against all odds—Mom become an LPN.

DURING THIS TIME, Mom was in a band. She sang, and she played guitar. It was neat to go to the shows and watch her perform. It was also neat to have the band at our house practicing so much—I played many a drum solo that absolutely no one bore witness to!

She even recorded a 45 record. And while other kids my age played records of their idols, my idol lived under the same roof as me.

I WAS A MOMMA'S GIRL—ATTACHED to her hip or under her feet at any given time.

I CAN REMEMBER when I was in the second grade and had been sick. I'd stayed home with Mom for several days. When it was time to go back to school, I took her notebook—something that she needed for her *own* studies. I took the notebook with me because I was so homesick, and every time I'd miss her, I'd go into the bathroom stall and look at her signature.

It didn't help me one bit because I'd cry and cry like I'd lost my best friend. And I guess I had.

Back at home, she was probably crying like she'd lost *her* best friend, too, because I know she needed that notebook.

EVEN THOUGH MY thoughts about school *never* changed throughout the years—never was a fan—I went on to graduate college, as did my brother, and sister.

I DON'T like telling that story about my Daddy because it makes me incredibly sad. And I didn't want to make that a part of Mom's story because it's so heartbreaking. But her story of triumph and perseverance can't be told without it.

WHILE SHE FACED tremendous heartache and hurdles along the way, a silver lining came about one day when she was introduced by to a fella named Clay by her friend, Sherry Turner.

THAT WAS a match made in Heaven.

HE DECIDED that he loved her enough to take on three kids he didn't make. It's not always easy to accept someone else's kids. Clay not only accepted us, but he loves us as if we were his own. And we love him right back.

MOM'S STORY of triumph doesn't stop at Prince Charming, though.

When she was in her forties, she went back to school once again and went on to become a Registered Nurse.

THE DAY I TURNED TWENTY-THREE, I thought about my mom and how different our lives were at that same age. I didn't know the first thing about living, but no one was relying on me, so I had plenty of time to figure it out.

Mom, at that age, had three babies under the age of five. She hadn't finished high school and had just lost her husband. She didn't have the luxury of time; She had to figure out life in an instant—baptism by fire.

MAYBE HER LIFE story can serve as an inspiration for others who may feel helpless and hopeless. Life can be unfair, as is spelled out here. It can also be a blessing, as is also spelled out here.

SOMETIMES THOSE BLESSINGS are slow to reveal themselves. But my hope is that they will come to you all . . .

28

BUZZ LIGHTYEAR, THE CANDY SLAYER

WHEN TYLER WAS THREE YEARS OLD, HE WENT TRICK-OR-TREATING IN the neighborhood. He wore a Buzz Lightyear costume and looked so stinkin' cute. Several neighbors had dropped off "special" treat bags at home before the festivities began.

Some neighbors give out one piece of candy; others give two. But some of us give treat bags. There are treat bags for just anyone which contain one's predetermined amount of candy. But special bags are set aside for favorite kids; they always include better candy and in bigger amounts. Such is life.

Anyway, we had given him candy at home, and with the bags the neighbors dropped off, he was off to a good start. He must have thought so, too.

We went to the first house. He walked up the sidewalk like a big boy, rang the doorbell, and waited. When the homeowner opened the door, he said, "Trick-or-Treat," just as we'd practiced. Then he opened his bag. When the neighbor went to put candy in his bag, Tyler declared, "I have enough." They couldn't believe their ears, and neither could we.

We moved along to the next house. Again, he walked to the door, rang the doorbell, said his rehearsed line, then told the homeowner that he had enough.

This pattern continued throughout the night. Some would respect his declaration, but most neighbors were so pleased with his honesty that they not only gave him the candy they had planned, but in several instances, they gave him more.

I don't know what we did to deserve such a wonderful child, but I sure am glad that God chose us to be his parents.

2 9

BUB'S ROOM

MY BROTHER, BEING FIVE YEARS OLDER THAN ME AND FOUR YEARS OLDER than our sister, didn't appreciate our presence in his room. But, we barged in every chance we could.

He had posters on his wall that scared me, so I tried to never go in there late in the evening because I'd think about them when I went to bed. His crime posters portrayed menacing looking individuals who were wielding guns. While I was raised in the country and firearms were certainly not a foreign concept, the actors holding them were terrifying to me. If that didn't keep me at bay, Bub's KISS posters did. I still remember Gene Simmons' big bloody tongue hanging out of his mouth in one of his rocker poses.

As Bub got older, he was given more freedom and was allowed to move his bedroom to the basement. With the posters being a thing of the past, I was unhampered in my exploration. He collected baseball cards and miniature batting helmets that sported team logos. He kept this stuff in a dresser drawer and on top of it, too. I loved to rummage through his loot.

He did not share my love and viewed it as an invasion of privacy. Sooo, he got himself a pet. I remember going in to plunder one day and getting the shock of my life. He had the biggest spider I had ever seen inside a jar on his nightstand. That kept me from crossing the threshold for a good long while!

One day, I came home from school on the bus. For some reason, neither Kim nor Bub were with me. I remember walking across the porch. Just before I walked through the entryway, I saw it. Right there beside me, in a jar, on the banister was that big black, *ugly*, nasty spider. I remember looking to the left and looking to the right. With no one around, I seized my opportunity. I hauled off —that's what we say in the country when something is about to get knocked the heck out—and hit that jar as hard as I could with my forearm, sending that mason jar sailing through the air. We had a huge bay window. It's a wonder I hadn't sent it sailing through that! Luckily, it flew toward the yard.

I cradled my books to my chest, threw my head back, and opened that front door like I was walking free from a jail cell.

I never admitted what I did to anyone at the time.

So, Bub, if you're reading this now, I'm sorry about your pet. And, Kim, if you're reading this, please accept my apology. I probably blamed it on you . . .

30

BIRD SOUP

When I was little, about three or four years old, I was walking in the hallway one day and overheard Mammaw tell someone on the phone that she'd killed two birds with one stone.

I remember my little head snapping to attention when she said that. Children take things literally, so I believed what I'd heard!

Later that day, she called me into the back room of her trailer - a built on addition, where she had a small kitchen area. I remember peeking up over the table and into an orange bowl filled with soup. My mind traveled back to the conversation earlier in the day. I peeked into the bowl again. It was creamy white with little chunks in it, and just exactly what I imagined bird soup must look like. Even though she said it was potato soup, I knew better. I knew what I'd heard!

Now that I'm grown up, I make potato soup for my own family. So, the next time I make a pot of "bird soup," I'll be killing two birds with one stone by filling our tummies with comfort food and also by reliving a memory of my precious Mammaw.

3 1

GRANNY CORA

EVERY SUMMER, AFTER SCHOOL WAS OUT, WE'D HEAD TO BEREA TO spend a week with Granny Cora.

WE ALWAYS HAD fun and filled our time with imaginative play. I remember Kim and I playing on the sidewalk. We'd play Mother May I, Red Light Green Light, and Leap Frog.

At night, we'd catch lightning bugs and sit on the porch.

I REMEMBER KIM, Bub, and me swinging on the swing set with Aunt Trick. We'd start off slow, then swing as high as we possibly could. Back and forth we'd go, laughing all the way. That is, until the jets flew over. For the life of me, I don't know why they flew so low. They seemed close enough to touch. And, they were loud as—well, as loud as a jet landing on your head.

It made no difference where I was when I heard them. No matter how high up, I'd jump. I'd jump and run for my life. As loud as they were, I never once heard them until they were right on top of my head.

. . .

ANOTHER TRIP, I spent an entire summer chasing birds through the yard with a salt shaker. Maybe two summers. It was explained to me that, if you could shake salt on a bird's tail, that you could catch it. Well, I dang sure wanted to do that, so off I'd go . . .

Granny and Grandpa's yard was every bit of forty acres, so I stayed busy—the intended purpose. If Fitbits existed back then, I would've broken records chasing birds and running from jets!

SOMETIMES WHEN WE showed up for our trip, there would be garbage bags filled with green beans on the porch. Like, Hefty bags. The black ones. I won't lie. That was a terrible sight. We'd work beans for ninety-seven of the twenty-four hours in a day. Okay, that's a slight exaggeration. But, to a kid, it felt like it took three years to work up one batch of beans. And I swear they had more than one!

With all the helpers, I'm sure it truly took no time at all.

I REMEMBER EATING Cheese Whiz with Uncle Jerry at the kitchen table. We'd never heard of Cheese Whiz, so it seemed delightful.

I remember granny making Sloppy Joes. The first time I ever had them was in Berea. I loved them.

I remember granny making spaghetti and meatballs. I remember bragging to my friends that my granny made bigger meatballs than they'd ever seen. I was certain they were the size of cabbages!

SPEAKING OF CABBAGE . . . Backing up a few years, Mom tells a story of taking us to Berea once. She said I was out of sorts and didn't want to stay. It had nothing to do with being at Granny's house. No, I just didn't want to leave my mommy. So, she said I looked at Granny and thought I'd try a little trash talk. She said I said, "Granny Cora, I'm gonna drive you up the wall!" She said Granny looked at me and said, "And, Amy, I'll drive you right through the floor!"

I'm guessing that was threat enough to straighten my back talkin' sassy self right up!

THE FIRST TIME I'd ever seen a blown glass vase was at Granny Cora's house. It sat on a built-in shelf in her living room, surrounded by precious family photos and the family Bible. One of those pictures on the ledge was of Granny's mother. She was a beautiful lady with dark hair and dark features. I remember thinking that she must be an Indian. Although, I don't think that was actually true.

Other pictures that stand out to me were graduation pictures of Aunt Trick, Uncle Jack, and Uncle Jerry.

Other pictures further up the wall, and ones that were dear to me, included pictures of my dad. One picture was of daddy and all his siblings. Aunt Trick was the only girl. She was accompanied in the picture by all my uncles - Joe, Jack, Eugene, Donnie, and Jerry. Daddy stood on the end, dressed in black from head to toe. This was his signature look.

My favorite picture was one of Daddy by himself. It was in a picture frame with a bubble glass front. The picture itself was a woodcarving with his photo overlaying the form. It had a 3-D feel to it. It always made me think of looking through a window, and in my little imagination, that's exactly what I was doing. It was like *seeing* him, not just a picture. It made me happy and sad all at the same time.

Back to the vase . . . The vase itself was multicolored, slim, and tall, holding colorful peacock feathers in varying shades of blue and green.

GRANNY CORA LOVED MUSIC. I don't think I fully grasped that as a kid. But she did. She played a banjo and had a really cool vintage guitar. If we'd beg hard enough, she'd bring them out, perch herself on the edge of the couch—the end near the hallway—and she'd play for us. We never dared ask if we could play. She did it so well, we knew our attempt would pale in comparison, anyway.

Granny had a console stereo in her living room—the kind that was about five feet long, solid wood construction, and with a hinged lid. When the lid was closed, a fancy little doily, a table lamp, and a candy dish sat on top of the radio. The candy dish was always filled with Creme Drops or jelly candy that looked like sugar coated orange slices.

Sometimes Granny would play vinyl records for us. At home, we had the 33s and the 45s, the big ones and little ones, respectfully. 33s were the size of a dinner plate, while the 45s were the size of a saucer.

The big ones, the 33s, had a full album of songs on it. The 45s had only a couple songs, and they were labeled as side A and side B. Side A had the most popular song. Side B was the equivalent of a B Movie; for all intents and purposes, they were not likely to be a sensation.

Anyway, when Granny started playing records for us, I quickly realized that there were also records that were 78s. They were midway between the sizes of a 33 LP and a 45. The 78s seemed thicker and heavier.

I thought I knew all there was to discover about music, so discovering a whole other size of record was super cool!

Granny loved George Jones. He was a handsome fella with amazing songs. I can see why the Possum was one of her favorites.

GRANNY WAS A SUPER NEAT HOUSEKEEPER. I never once recall anything being out of place. She ran a tight ship where everything had its place.

She was also very giving. Anytime we left her house, we left with food, toiletries, or cleaning supplies. It was like going to the store. She had these little metal storage cabinets that she kept stocked with a variety of food and other staples. She also had a metal building that was filled with freezers. We'd always take a trip out there before heading home, too. We felt guilty taking the things she offered because we didn't want her to be without. It made her happy to give us things. As I've gotten older, I understand that a little better.

. . .

GRANNY WAS one of those mountain women who didn't put up with nonsense. If you messed around her house at night, you were greeted with a shotgun.

The gun probably weighed more than she did. Still yet, a trespasser wouldn't have faired so well had they stumbled onto her property with ill intent!

REMEMBER that forty acre yard that I spoke of? It may have been an acre at most. But it seemed absolutely huge to me—at least a mile from the porch to the road.

That little black and white trailer still sits just off the road on Highway 1016. I drove by it the other day, for old times' sake. It brought back a flood of wonderful memories.

Many more homes surround it now, and time has moved on. Still yet, I could almost hear the laughter ring out as I imagined three little Pennington kids frolicking through the yard in another era.

AND, remember that super cool vintage guitar that Granny Cora used to play? Well, it's now mine and is proudly displayed in the corner of my dining room. Anytime I need to remember, just the strum of a chord brings back a mountain of memories . . .

3 2

SATURDAY MORNING FORTS

Saturday mornings at our house weren't filled with social media and video games. I grew up in a simpler time in the seventies and eighties. While we were blessed with modern conveniences of the era, imagination was still a big part of growing up. We made our own fun, as I heard my little Mammaw say so many times about her own childhood. And, in making our own fun, creative play was a necessity.

As soon as the cartoons went off, it was time to find something to do. The "something" that we often chose was to make forts. We'd drag all the kitchen chairs into the hallway. The hallway was a long dark corridor separating the kitchen and living room. After placing the chairs where we wanted them, we'd then go into the bedrooms, just off the hallway, and strip the beds of every drop of cover. We'd drag those blankets, sheets, bedspreads, afghans, quilts—whatever happened to be serving as bedding at the moment—and we'd drape them over the chairs. Half the fun, or most of the fun, of building Saturday Morning Forts was the actual building process. Everything had to line up just so because we all know that forts have to be pitch black inside. Any sliver of light filtering in ruins the covert operation and just won't do. Once the fort was erected to our satisfaction, we'd crawl inside. To be honest, this is when the game stopped being fun, so we'd quickly move on to the next adventure.

Tearing down the fort wasn't nearly as fun as building it, but then again, cleanup is always the hard part.

I'm glad I grew up in a time where imaginations ran wild, in a time where simplicity wasn't a bad thing.

Maybe that's responsible for this old soul I seem to have . . .

33

STRINGING UP BEANS

MY HUSBAND AND I HAD BEEN MARRIED A COUPLE OF YEARS WHEN WE decided we were gonna grow a garden. A big one. My little Mammaw came up to visit, and I couldn't wait to take her out to the garden. I had spent the day before stringing up bean vines and making them look just so. They looked like I'd seen other peoples' gardens look, so I was pretty dang satisfied with my efforts.

Mammaw and I trotted out to the garden. I pointed out my beans right away and commented how pretty they looked. A *huge* grin spread across her face. She, too, agreed they looked pretty. Then she added, "But they're not bean vines." Apparently, I had spent my time stinging up morning glories or something other than what I intended.

And that's just ok. It's stories like that that I think back on and, they always make me laugh.

34

A JUMBLE OF MEMORIES

ON ANY WINTER DAY, BACK IN THE 1970S AND EIGHTIES, MOM MADE US homemade hot chocolate out of Hershey's Cocoa. It was the best hot chocolate ever, and I still make it to this day, despite modern conveniences.

Now, Tyler makes it, too.

I LOVED WHEN MY COUSIN, Jenny, came for a visit because she always made popcorn balls for us. In my mind, they were as big as the moon. But reality tells me they were *just* a tad smaller.

MY MOM CAN MAKE the best fried chicken in Kentucky, hands down. You've heard of Kentucky Fried Chicken. Well, honey, the Colonel ain't got nothing on my Momma! I love her chicken more than anything. She makes it like Granny Maggard did—with a whole lotta love, a whole lotta salt, and a whole lotta lard. God bless a southern cook!

. . .

MAMMAW MADE the best cornbread in the world. The universe, even. What I wouldn't give for a warm slice straight from the oven. I have the flour, the cornmeal, the milk, and the cast iron skillet. I have all the tools, but it will never be hers.

Actually, that's not completely true. Mammaw used Three Rivers Cornmeal. They no longer make that. I'd like to say that's why my cornbread tastes different. But I know that's not true.

MY AUNT VERA made the very best banana pudding that I've ever eaten. In our family, we make banana pudding with vanilla pudding. We just prefer that flavor over the banana type.

Anyway, the last time I made Aunt Vera's pudding, I was in a hurry and slung together the ingredients pretty haphazardly. I told Mom that I could feel Aunt Vera's spirit standing beside me saying, "That's not what I said to do!" It made us chuckle.

MY UNCLE EUGENE made the best gingerbread I've ever eaten. I tried to make it using his recipe. It's just not the same.

Still yet, I can imagine him smiling down on us because he knew we loved his food so good!

MY AUNT TRICK makes the best dumplings, turkey and dumplings. They are simply divine.

One might think that I'm hungry as I write this. One might be correct in that assumption.

I CAN REMEMBER BEING on the phone with my cousin, Teresa, one day. I was about five. I was standing in the kitchen looking out the window. She asked me what I was doing. I told her that I was chewing grape bubblegum.

I said, "Smell." I pulled my gum out of my mouth and held it to the mouthpiece.

She giggled and gently explained that she couldn't smell through the phone.

That memory always makes me smile when it crosses my mind.

MAMMAW ALWAYS PUT TOGETHER TREAT bags for Halloween. I enjoyed helping her. Sometimes she'd make ghost suckers—a lollipop with a Kleenex over it. Orange or black yarn was tied around the base of the lollipop, and then we'd draw a smiley face on it. She also liked to jot down how many ghosts and goblins she had and the costumes they wore.

Now that I'm grown up, every Halloween, Bru, Tyler, and I make treat bags. The last count was two hundred and fifty. It's never enough, and we never make it through the second hour. For me, it's more about remembering my little Mammaw and the tradition she started all those years ago.

BOOSE TAUGHT me to ride a bike. Like every other teacher since the invention of the bicycle, she coached me to get on, then said she'd hold on all the way.

Once I started going, I turned back to say, "I'm doing it!" It was exhilarating, and I was proud. When I looked back, she was at the propane tank, halfway down the driveway from me. She'd let go. Scared, I wrecked my bike immediately.

She encouraged me to get back on it. When I told her I couldn't do it, she reminded me that I was doing it when I thought she was steadying me.

As fate would have it, there's been many times in my life when I thought I couldn't do something. And, just like those Hurricane Creek days, my little cheerleader has been right there for me—guiding me at first—then letting go so I can see for myself that I really can do it.

· · ·

GROWING UP, we always made popcorn on the stove, the old fashioned way. It was a prerequisite for card night. I learned to play Canasta at a young age. Before the Internet and twenty-four hour kid TV, you did what the grownups did. And the grownups in my family played cards. If there was a group, they played Canasta, Pinochle, and Polish Rummy—which is a Phase 10 type game. If there was no one around, they played Solitaire.

Now that I'm grown up, I still make old fashioned popcorn on the stove and still play cards.

As for the next generation, *my* son now plays Canasta. When he was little, he'd build card houses, just like I used to.

Keeping with tradition, I passed that skill on to my next to youngest nephew when I taught him to do the same.

I TAUGHT my niece and nephew to play War with cards, just like the kids in my family did growing up.

WHEN MY NEXT TO youngest niece was three years old, I taught her to play See See My Playmate - a hand clapping game that Kim taught me, and Lori taught her.

It's something that we still can do today. But, we laugh so hard, no one knows what we're even saying. Then we have to pee. I'm not even ashamed to say that. Everyone needs that level of laughter in their life!

Now that my youngest niece has shown an interest in learning See See My Playmate, I'm starting to show her.

TRADITIONS DON'T HAVE to be elaborate to be special. Sometimes it's simply a nod to simpler times. And we could all use simple times sometimes.

3 5

AUNTS AND UNCLES

AUNT AUDREY AND UNCLE BEN

It was Springtime, 1970 something, and we had gone down to my Aunt Audrey and Uncle Ben's house. As we walked away, I noticed how beautiful her Easter flowers were at the end of her house. We didn't have *any* at our house, and I was positive she wouldn't miss a few.

Sooo, I lagged behind the others and swiped a bouquet before leaving the driveway.

I got home and put them in a glass, displaying them prominently on the TV so Mom could appreciate her giant bouquet of daffodils all night long. Couldn't miss them if she tried.

Fast forward to that evening . . .

We got word that some hooligan had busted out of our local jail. These people always seemed to end up on Hurricane Creek. I have no idea why. I also have no idea if that's an accurate memory. But, for some reason, that's how I recall it.

Back to the story . . .

Anyway, for some reason, my aunt was home alone, and Mom insisted that she come to our house.

I would've walked that woman to any house on the creek or even stood watch over her *myself* at her house—any house—but ours.

You see, that criminal and I had one thing in common that evening - we were both sweating bullets that we'd get caught!

Aunt Audrey came to the house that evening. There the flowers were, prominently displayed on our giant floor model television . . . where she couldn't have possibly missed them if she tried! The night wore on, my guilt mounting down on me like a winepress!

No one caught sight of the criminal that night on Hurricane Creek. Well, not the one that broke out of jail, anyway. The resident criminal was there for everyone to see. But, by the grace of God, Aunt Audrey didn't mention the flowers nor the striking resemblance they bore to the ones that so prominently graced her flowerbed at the end of their house.

It was a good lesson for me. I didn't steal Easter flowers again until I was an adult and borrowed some off Granny's hill to transplant here so I'd have a little bit of Hurricane Creek outside my own front door.

AUNT PAT and Uncle Rich

We used to spend a lot of time up at Aunt Pat and Uncle Rich's house. I always enjoyed being on their porch and playing with all the cousins that congregated there.

They always had the neatest things like an Atari, tons of board games, and barbie dolls. But the memories that stand out the most aren't even about toys. No, after forty years, I can still remember the smell of their conditioner. Finesse was the brand, and I've never smelled anything better. The second thing that impressed my little self back in the seventies was that Aunt Pat had Dixie cups in the bathroom and a little dispenser that held them.

When I grew up and had a child of my own, I bought Dixie Cups for his bathroom. And, if they still make those little cups when he has kids, just maybe they'll be in their bathroom.

Another thing that stands out to me was Aunt Pat's candy dish. She always had cinnamon candy and butterscotch discs in the same container.

Now that I'm all grown up, if I buy candy, I buy them both. I enjoy seeing that gold and crimson mingling together in the same container and reminding me of the 1970s on Hurricane Creek.

It's funny the things in life that shape you. We have so many traditions, both big and small, that leave imprints on our hearts. You never know what the next generation will take away from knowing you. I look forward to the discovery.

UNCLE DAVE and Aunt Helen

Uncle Dave and Aunt Helen lived down the road between Uncle Ben and Aunt Pat. I enjoyed visiting. Aunt Helen was the first one to ever make Hamburger Helper for me. I thought that was the best stuff ever! I still remember eyeing the box on the table. It had the little Hamburger Helper guy with his little white glove body.

The first time I saw bunk beds was at their house. That piqued my interest greatly.

We only had twin beds at our house. But that wasn't a problem; I knew they could be made into bunk beds.

One day, I headed down the road to play. Before I left, I left a note for Mom that I wanted our twin beds converted into bunk beds. A simple modification would've done the trick! I could see it clearly in my head. I pictured the top surface of the bottom bedposts to be notched out to form little buttons. The underside of the top bunk posts would have holes that the buttons would perfectly fit in. I did all the engineering, the hard part. All they had to do was do it.

So I left the note about the miracle bunk beds and also requested that our room be clean when I got back. It was a mess.

I can tell you that I was astonished when I came home and none of that business had happened! Truly astonished!

But, I digress . . .

I loved going to Boose's because it was always so much fun. When they lived in town, we'd play our badminton guitars in the yard. Boose and Missy would put a stereo speaker in the upstairs window, Joan Jett spilling from the speakers. We'd sing, "I love Rock-n-Roll" to the top of our lungs, all the while putting on a show to passersby on the Spur.

Once they moved back to Hurricane, we had big fun again with prank calls and sleepovers in the Poutin' House, our attempts at learning to play guitar, all night videos with us camped out in the living room—just lots of wonderful memories at their house.

Uncle Dave was incredibly talented. He was a mechanic, a wood-worker, a musician, and a songwriter. He made his mark on Bluegrass music, co-writing the iconic bluegrass tune, "Lefty's Old Guitar."

UNCLE PAUL

I remember the smell of Uncle Paul's pipe and how Mammaw and Granny looked forward to his and Aunt Mel's visits because that's the only time they got to play Pinocle. Uncle Paul and Aunt Mel were very giving, graciously allowing tagalongs on their many vacations.

I remember telling Aunt Mel that Uncle Paul looked just like Vincent Price—only, Uncle Paul was more handsome.

UNCLE ED

I remember the laughter that Uncle Ed could so easily evoke from everyone with his silly demeanor. He was a truly funny guy who loved to fish and grow a big garden.

When I was in high school, he married Aunt Carrie—bringing Jarod and Nicole into our lives.

The moment I met Nicole, we were instant bffs—inseparable! So much so, on one visit, I had to go to school, and I took her with me. The teacher didn't notice at first. Halfway through class, she stopped the lecture, pinned Nicole with a perplexed glare, and finally asked, "Are you in my class?" We've laughed over that for years.

As for other Amy & Nicole stories, that's where this must end! There was that ring story, though . . .

. . .

Aunt Leona

I remember how skilled Aunt Leona was at reupholstering Granny's furniture. Even as a child, I was amazed at her talent. She could take something old and bring new life to it with some fresh fabric and her keen skill.

I loved going to North Carolina to visit her and Uncle Brutus. We ate like kings on those trips.

I remember a clock that Uncle Brutus had when they lived down in South Port. It indicated high tide and low tide. It was simple, but I thought it was super neat.

When I look back at Aunt Leona's pictures, I think she looks like a dark haired Marilyn Monroe.

This talented lady can sing, sew, woodwork, and so much more. She has a super kind spirit—the kind that warms your heart and draws you near.

Aunt Meff

Aunt Meff has always been so well spoken and poised. She was the driving force in getting the Runaway Truck Ramp installed at the foot of the Hyden Spur, which has a steep grade that would test the limits of a passenger car, not to mention a coal truck or semi.

I'm sure no one at home knows that, but she's saved many lives because of her forward thinking and perseverance.

She knows I love stories, and she always has one to tell me when we talk.

She's a great source of inspiration to me, always encouraging me to continue with my writing, and filling my spirit with positivity.

Uncle Eddie

I remember being at Uncle Eddie's house once when I was little. We were sitting down for supper. We had steak. I'm not sure how I remember that because what follows should have kept me from remembering anything!

Anyway, Uncle Eddie had broken his toe. I was the last one to the table. I'm not sure how it happened, but I managed to sit in the chair, skid it across, and land it firmly—all at the same time—straight onto his toe. *His very broken toe!*

That was 1980 something. I remember sitting down to the table, and now it's today. I don't remember a thing in between!

When he's not bellering at me for re-breaking his already broken phalanges, Uncle Eddie is a talented singer, songwriter, and guitar picker—a prevalent talent in our family. He's also an electrician.

Uncle Eugene

I remember Uncle Eugene taking us lots of places when we were little. One time, he took us bowling. To say I was a terrible bowler was an understatement.

When it was my turn to bowl, I focused my sights, swung my arm back, and propelled that ball forward. I knew it might not be a strike, but I was gonna take down some pins! Somehow, I managed to hit the gutter wide open. My ball careened down that rutted out path, hopped the edge, and sailed into another lane.

There was a league in the next lane over, and I had just joined their competition. If they didn't manage a strike with two balls rolling toward the pins, they sure couldn't blame me!

I'm not sure either party was proud of my skills that day. But, I guarantee that I'm the star of that bowling league's story when they ask, "Remember that time . . .?"

Aunt Trick

I can remember Aunt Trick bringing Granny Cora to Hyden to come get us when we were little. Seems like she drove a little red car, but I can't be certain of that.

It was always fun to have her in our town because we usually saw her in Berea.

When we were teenagers, she used to take us shopping and to church.

It wasn't until I was older that I remember having her dumplings. And I *know* I've already mentioned her dumplings, but they are D-E-L-I-C-I-O-U-S!

Bru had surgery once. And, Aunt Trick being Aunt Trick, she sprang into action and made a big batch of dumplings for me! Ahem, I mean him.

Wonder if I can talk him into another surgery for the sole purpose of getting comfort food—for his wife?

Uncle Jack

I remember something that my Uncle Jack said to everyone when I was little. I can't clearly recall if he had brought a video camera to granny's or if he had someone there videoing.

I remember a whole slew of Pennington family being there. We were all ducking and dodging and trying to stay out of the way of the camera.

Finally, he pointed out that, one day, we'd wish we had those pictures and videos.

It was good advice. It's still good advice and something that I've never forgotten.

We have to be purposeful in preserving memories.

Uncle Donnie

I remember us going four wheeling with Uncle Donnie. He had a blue Jeep. I can remember going up in Short Fork, bouncing all over the place because the path was so broken, and having so much fun.

I remember crying the day I found out that Uncle Donnie was moving. We always loved going to his house and having them at ours.

Once I grew up, and had a child of my own, fate would send us on a college tour to the very town that my uncle moved to all those years before.

We had a wonderful visit with him and Kim; the food was fantastic, the football game was great, the college tour that Kim gave us was phenomenal, and the memories we made that weekend will last us a lifetime.

UNCLE JERRY

I can remember Uncle Jerry and how handsome he was. He was cool with his music preferences. In those days, I hated country music. Uncle Jerry was more of a southern rock lover—which was more in line with what we liked. He was closer in age to Bub, so many times, it was more like having another brother than another uncle.

I remember Uncle Jerry taking me to the Pinnacles in Berea. I was in my early teens. We hiked up the mountain, both of us sweating like Pennington's. At one point, I got off the path—I still can't fathom how this happened. Anyway, I was *not* dressed for hiking. I was dressed for seeing a cute boy.

I don't know if I didn't hear Uncle Jerry when he said where we were going, or if I just didn't know what the Pinnacles were. All I know is that I was wearing my "Jesus shoes," as he dubbed them. They were strappy sandals that crisscrossed over my ankles and tied up on my leg.

Anyway, I was off the path. I was afraid I'd fall and kill myself trying to get back on that steep incline with my "hiking shoes," so I thought I'd jump.

Only, I didn't have the courage to do that. He'd try to coax me down as gently as possible, but fear anchored me to my spot.

He was hot, tired, and running out of time when he finally said, "You HAVE to come down! You been up there forty-five minutes. I'm gonna be late for work!"

And, honestly, I don't recall how I got down.

I remember holding on to a flimsy tree; and now it's today. I don't recall a thing in between.

. . .

UNCLE JOE

I remember Uncle Joe and his many visits to our house on Hurricane. We were always happy to see him come over. Sometimes he'd stay a little later than our bedtime, and we always liked that because we'd get to stay up later to visit with him.

Whether it be birthday gifts, sharing garden veggies, or simply stopping in to say hello, he was always very giving and kind. He reminded me a lot of Grandpa.

36

SNOW WARNING

I'VE LIVED IN RICHMOND FOR TWENTY-SEVEN YEARS NOW - IN CITY limits, mind you. So the possibility of getting stranded for days is not very likely anymore. However, when faced with an impending snow-storm, I still feel the need to hit the store wide open. Yes. I'm one of "those" people. You can take the girl out of the holler, but you can't take the holler out of the girl . . .

37

SMOKING HOT DEAL

WHILE RESEARCHING VACATION RENTALS IN OUR PRICE RANGE, something popped up as an option that made my sister and me laugh until we cried. It was a three story beach house, oceanfront, and fully ablaze. Yes. The flames reached the heavens and so did our laughter when we saw *exactly* what the rental company thought we could afford. Can't make this stuff up!

3 8

UNSPOKEN RULE OF THE SOUTH

IF SOMEONE GIVES YOU A BREAK IN TRAFFIC TO MAKE YOUR TURN, YOU toss up your hand and wave.

PLAIN AND SIMPLE.

IF YOU BREAK THAT RULE, you just might cause a good Southern girl to lose her charm.

39

THE EYE DOCTOR

April 8, 2015

I have Tyler at the eye doctor. I can't even make eye contact with him or the doctor because I'm reminded of an eye doctor appointment from when I was a child.

Mammaw had taken me to the eye doctor so I could see about getting contact lenses. The doctor was up in my face - as in, we were so close, our eyelashes could've fluttered against one another. He was staring intently into my eyes when I felt it coming on. I tried biting my lips together to hold my mouth shut. No go. Once that hint of laughter got rolling, there was simply no stopping it. The ripple started in my stomach and didn't stop until I was in full on hysterical cackling!

He'd back away, and I'd regain my composure . . . until he came at me again. I didn't even have visible eyes at that point! What I did have we're eyes that were slammed shut, a mouth that was gaping open, and an unrestrained giggling fit that could be heard all throughout the office. I just couldn't "Straighten Up!" no matter how many times Mammaw directed that order at me!

. . .

EVEN THOUGH I'LL never forget that doctor's appointment, I sure picked a real bad time to remember it.

40

TEACHER APPRECIATION

During Teacher Appreciation week, don't forget to thank your favorite teachers or share an unforgettable memory. I have a few that stand out:

Ms. Howard for giving us nap time in kindergarten. I'm sure I fussed something fierce, but it gave me mad life skills. I'm an excellent napper now.

Miss Jean for taking all us first graders to her house for a field trip where we picnic'd under the Pines. I can still remember the smell of the grass. Anytime I smell that now, I'm instantly transported back in my mind to that little hillside where the sun was filtering down through the trees. Even though we were just a few steps from the school, my memory says we were deep in the forest on a grand adventure. It was big stuff!

Mrs. Roark for reading us the Boxcar Children. Forty years later, I still remember one of the scenes that my little imagination conjured up while she read to us.

IN FOURTH GRADE, Mrs. Caldwell spanked me nearly every day for talking. She'd turn my hand palm up, bend my fingers down, and whack the dickens out of my wrist and open hand. She once introduced me to "Black Betsy," a big, black rubber paddle with holes drilled in it - I learned to curb my tongue that day. What doesn't kill you makes you stronger, right?

IN SIXTH GRADE, Mrs. Raye Mosley let us put items in a time capsule. I think we wrote some stuff, too. Wonder where that thing is and hoping I said something more profound than, "I love Michael Jackson, and Twynell does, too!"

GOING OUT OF ORDER, but my senior year in high school, I had Sharon Mosley. I was terrified of that woman. But it didn't take long to realize I'd met my favorite teacher because it was in her class that I developed a love for English and writing.

IN SEVENTH GRADE, Mr. Onzie Feltner allowed me to live after catching me with gum for the umpteenth time. On this day, I didn't have any backup gum, so I only spit half of it out once he instructed me to get rid of it. I returned to my seat, continued talking to my gang - Boose, Rachel, Twynell, Cindy and Susie - got lost in the moment, and started chewing again. That's when we heard, "PENNINGTON!" Every head in the class snapped up to look at him, then to me. "What's that in your mouth?" he asked. That was real bad because I didn't have any more gum, and I knew he'd make me spit it out. It got worse when he told me to go to the hallway. Only bad kids went to the hallway. And you went to the hallway for one reason and one reason only—to be spanked. Sure enough, he followed me out, paddle in hand. <sigh> He told me to face the wall, so I did. I clenched my eyes shut and waited for the fire to hit my behind. I heard it first—a loud, echoing thud. I braced myself for the pain that was sure to split me apart. But it never came. I opened my eyes and looked at Mr. Feltner. The paddle was against the wall, the one that was between us and the classroom. He smiled at me and dared me to tell anyone that he hadn't actually spanked me, that he'd only hit the wall.

Years later, after I'd grown up, I went home to the Mary Breckinridge Festival. I was looking at a craft booth when I heard a voice behind me ask, "PENNINGTON! What's that in your mouth?" I smiled and turned to see that sweet teacher that did not give me what I deserved on that day way back when at Hyden Elementary.

I'M NOT sure this was his most shining moment, but it's one that sure was memorable for me. When I was a sophomore in high school, Mr. Morgan said something to me that I will never forget. I was in World Civ class. I promise I was asking a classmate for clarification on something when a booming voice sounded from the front of the class. It was Mr. Morgan, and he had caught me talking for the umpteenth time! He said, "Amy Pennington, you have diarrhea of the mouth; it never does quit running!" So, as I eluded, maybe not his most endearing moment, but daggone if I haven't laughed over that for years! And so has my sister.

WHEN I WAS a senior in high school, I was in chorus class. Miss Bass was our teacher. I was in the Alto group. When you sing in a group, that safety in numbers gives you a little more courage to sing out. It all blends together and dilutes individual mistakes.

There was one day that we had to go up, two by two. Miss Bass was playing the piano, and my classmate and I had to sing our parts. Solo. As we stood there with our backs to the class, I wanted to crawl under that piano because being in the spotlight has never been my comfort zone. The class wasn't listening. But she was.

The song was, "I Will Sing a Song for a Russian Child." With all the courage I could muster, I sang my part. She stopped playing, looked up at me, and said, "You have a beautiful voice." I wanted to cry. It still makes me cry, actually.

I'm sure I batted that compliment away with some self-deprecating humor because—well, because that's who I am and always have been. And, while I know that those words of affirmation likely seemed unappreciated, she'll never know how they stuck with me.

I HAVE a ton of other stories, but I think I'll stop there.

TO ALL YOU teachers out there, you are special people who provide valuable skills and leave lasting memories on every student that crosses your path. You're what we country folk would call "Good People." Thanks for being your wonderful selves and planting seeds of greatness into generations of kids who may not have always seemed to appreciate the effort.

4 1

FALLEN ANGEL

SOME OF MY EARLIEST TEACHINGS OF JESUS CHRIST OCCURRED AT THE
Mary Breckinridge house located on Wendover in Hyden, Kentucky.
The "Big House," as it was known was a two-story log cabin that sat
atop a tree-dotted mountain overlooking the murky waters of the
Middle Fork River.

For those of you who don't know the legacy of Mary Breckinridge,
she and her team of midwives traveled throughout rural Appalachia
on horseback. They did so to provide healthcare to families in an
effort to decrease the high incidence of infant and maternal deaths
during childbirth.

So, she was in the business of helping birth babies at home.

Mary Breckinridge and her team stored new babies in the saddle-
bags that were draped across the horses and took them to eager and
exhausted families when the time was just right. Well, that's not
exactly how it worked, but in 1955 when my mom was five years old
and waiting for a baby that her mom was to "get," that's how she
thought it worked. She would impatiently wait for the nurses to arrive
on horseback with her little brother or sister, and every time when
they would leave, there was no baby–even though the saddle bags still
appeared to be full of babies since they were bulging. One day she said

to my Mammaw, "Mommy, if they don't have a baby for you next time, tell them you're tired of fooling with them!"

FAST FORWARD TO WINTER 1970 something when my family and I trekked down to the Big House.

EVERY CHRISTMAS we put on a production of the Christmas story depicting Jesus' birth. This one particular year my brother, Tony, was Joseph, and my cousin, Tina, was Mary. I don't recall who were the wise men, the innkeeper, or even the little animals, but if they were there, I'm sure they were family.

The rest of us little darlings were angels. Let me say, I was a fine angel. However, I had sticky fingers. During rehearsals, I saw baby Jesus just lying there in the manger all alone. No one was playing with him. No one was holding him or talking to him. So *perhaps* Mary Breckinridge was channeling through me because I got up from my little angel throne and got him. I was just trying to nurture. I got baby Jesus right out of that little crib; I held him, and I talked to him. Then I talked a lot more when those big meanies stole baby Jesus right out from under my nose! They took him away and put him back in that lonely bed. I won't rehash, but baby Jesus was *m-i-n-e*. Well, not technically, but no one else was playing with him, so I didn't see why it would be a problem if I did.

Hmmpt! They had other ideas. *No one* was coming around to my way of thinking. I sat there during practice, the distraught angel.

The night of the play had arrived. All the parents piled in and packed the room. The performance began. We depicted the story perfectly—well, except for the little devil-angel that was about to shake things up.

We've all seen the other plays where the kids line up holding their 'M-E-R-R-Y C-H-R-I-S-T-M-A-S' letter signs, one per kid. Where you see one child who has their letter upside down. You know how much *that* would stand out? Everyone would just watch, and laugh, and not have the heart to say anything. My story was something like that . . . only different.

So, as I said, the story was depicted with astonishing accuracy–only we had twins. There were two sweet baby Jesus'—the one in the manger and the other one I had so I'd leave baby Jesus alone. They had to give me a baby so that I wouldn't *steal* baby Jesus during the performance!

But alas, my acting debut was short lived. Before I was dragged off stage - Yes. I said *dragged*. I noticed that my brother, "Joseph," looked a little . . . different. He was wearing something that he never wore at home. It was a towel with a cord tied around it-on his head-in public! Soooo, in a muffled voice, I'm sure, I said, "Bub, get that thing off your head. Get that thing off your head, Bub!" I rose to my feet to assist with the request when they struck. They, the big meanies, hadn't given me the opportunity to spot my cousin Tina. I mean, "Mary's," headdress because I was gone!

You know how in old movies how they show people being dragged off the stage with a hook, like the curvy part of a cane? My exit was just as obvious. I was *dragged* off the stage by my feet. My halo probably shot sparks they pulled me off so fast! Mom had one foot, and someone that I don't recall through the blur had my other foot. Perhaps it was Sharon Kosher.

I was then banished to a room. Where's the Christmas spirit in that, I ask? So there I sat, on a bed, all alone - just me and my Jesus twin. I remember staring at a puddle on the floor until the play was over. I imagine that the puddle was from melted snow because we always had big snows back then.

After the play, the real fun began. I was allowed back into the room with everyone else. (Oh my goodness, it's just dawned on me that I was in solitary confinement at the age of four! Thank you, Lord, for the ability to reform.)

So after the traditional stuff you know, MJ and the twins - we got to see Santa. He came there every year. We'd sit on his lap and tell him what we wanted for Christmas. He always pulled out a wrapped toy from his bag. It was never what we asked for, but it was the best toy ever, anyway. After that, we went to the window and got hot chocolate. It was sooo hot, I'm surprised our kids have taste buds!

The hot chocolate warmed our bones, just like this memory warms my heart. I absolutely loved the Christmas programs at the Big House and the lasting memories that were gained there.

4 2

THE HOME VISIT

THIS STORY IS ONE OF MOM'S. WHEN SHE WAS LITTLE, THE FNS NURSES would make home visits. The nurse would come to one house, and all the neighborhood kids would go there to see her to receive their immunizations.

When it was time for Mom to receive *her* shot, she ran and slid under a bed that was against the wall. She scooted all the way up against the wall so they couldn't pull her out.

They'd finally tired of her antics and decided to move the bed to get to her. Only, when they pulled the bed out, she wasn't there. Well, she was *there;* they just couldn't see her. The bed she was under had open box springs, which meals the coils were exposed. So, she hooked her fingers and toes in the springs. When they moved the bed, she went with it. This continued a few times before they finally crawled up under there with her and gave her the shot, anyway!

I can only imagine the laughs that that little Lovett girl, my Momma, caused that day on Hurricane Creek!

43

MATH

THIS IS A STORY THAT'S NOT MY OWN, BUT ONE I ALWAYS ENJOYED hearing. It was one of Mammaw's favorites from her teaching days on Hurricane Creek.

Mammaw was doing a math lesson one day and told the students that one plus three equaled four. She said, "I had this little feller who sat back and stared at me. He set his mouth just so, then he said, 'Now, listen, Mister. Two plus two is four!'" She got a good laugh out of that when she told it. She said that she told him he was right, but showed him how one plus three was also four.

44

THE POSSUM

Bru and I cleaned out the dryer vent that goes up underneath the house. We also cleaned the bendy tube—technical, I know—that attaches to the dryer. When we got everything back in place and turned the dryer on, that tube jumped and jerked like a critter was in it and trying to break free. It wasn't. This time.

Years ago, when we first got married, we lived in an apartment the size of a motel room. Maybe smaller than that. No kidding. We barely had room for us, so we sure didn't have room for a washer and dryer.

One weekend Mom and Clay were out of town, so we went over to do laundry. All. Weekend. Long.

On Friday, after feeding their dog, I went outside after seeing him standing there staring at his food. Then I saw why. A possum was eating his food. I tried to shoo it away. It looked up from eating and hissed at me. Hissed. But it didn't do it twice!

I picked up a wrench as big as a broom handle, give or take an inch, and I threw it at the possum-not to hit it, but to scare it away. Being the brave one I was, I did this while running away. And scream-ing. I might've cried a little . . .

All weekend, with every load of laundry, the dryer stunk worse and worse. It was horrific. I left a note for Mom that there was something *bad* wrong with her dryer, that the smell would knock you down!

Turns out, when I threw that wrench at that hissing, creepy creature, I did hit it. And to exact its revenge, it crawled into the dryer vent, where I cooked its hiney all weekend long.

Ahhh, memories. Some are sweeter than others . . .

45

SCHOOL FORMS

Every year when school starts back, like most parents, we fill out paperwork. Not just any paperwork, but the kind that makes your hand cramp you've been filling them out so long paperwork. You know the kind. Right?

So, we're about halfway through the packet when we come across the home language survey. Question: "What language is most commonly spoken at home?"

I'm tired, cranky, crampy, and answer the first thing that enters my mind, "Sarcasm."

My husband took over the paperwork.

46

GUM

WHEN I WAS LITTLE, AROUND SIX OR SEVEN, I WENT TO BED ONE NIGHT with gum in my mouth. Now, when I chewed gum, I liked bubblegum. And I always chewed two pieces. Two.

So, not wanting to spit my gum out, I went to bed with it still in my mouth.

THE NEXT MORNING, Mom received a phone call at work—a distress phone call.

"AMY'S STUCK TO THE WALL."

ALARMED, she questioned the caller. "Whaddaya mean 'Amy's stuck to the wall'?"

· · ·

117

"JUST WHAT I SAID. She's stuck. To the wall!"

MOM CAME HOME EARLY from the hospital, and sure enough, I was stuck to the wall.

IN THE MIDDLE of the night, that wad of gum had come out of my mouth and tangled in my hair. At some point, I'd nestled in a little too close to the wall—and there I'd stay until daylight hours when I awoke to them cutting me loose.

47

FAT LADY

WHEN KIM AND I WERE LITTLE, WE PLAYED A GAME WE CALLED FAT Lady. In Mammaw's trailer, the heat vents were in the floor. We would stand over the vents and wait. When the heat kicked on, it would flare out our floor-length gowns. We would raise the roof in hysterics because we were Fat Ladies.

As ADULTS, that Fat Lady game ain't so endearing.

4 8

HAIR MISHAPS

I'D LIKE TO SHARE MY TWO CENTS ABOUT HAIR SITUATIONS. WE'VE ALL had them, that moment in time when we imagined one thing in our mind and saw a totally different thing on our head. Maybe the stylist stayed out a little late the night before the appointment. Maybe the stylist thought something else would look better on our heads and made a creative choice. *Or* maybe the stylist was your sister, and you had to go to Kimberly Scissorhands in an effort to save money. Nevertheless, I have many stories to tell, and somewhere, a few pictures to prove it! So let's get started . . .

WHEN I WAS about two years old, I visited the resident hair stylist/mutilator. Actually, I probably had no choice but to sit there and have the "conditioning pack" applied. Mom came down the hall and overheard Kim, in her toddler lingo, say, "Let me osh it one more time, Amy." Mom came into the bathroom to find that Kim had applied almost an entire tub of Vaseline to my hair. As you can imagine, that cannot be washed out. So, Mom and Mammaw each worked on my hair trying to rub the excess out with towels. After numerous washes, Mom said that my once thin tabby hair was full and thick. I'm sure that's called product buildup, but it was a miracle!

WHEN KIM and I were about three and four, we decided to cut each other's hair. I'm sure it was little dictator's idea because, as I have mentioned before, I was the baby and a perfect child! Anyway, Kim went first. I remember that we were sitting on our dresser/chest. As I have also mentioned before, I don't know the difference. We were sitting on the long one. So Kim had cut my hair right to my scalp in places. Hmm. This was a prelude of things to come . . . Then it was my turn to do the cutting. This was when Mom came down the hall and saw long strands of hair everywhere and heard me talking about cutting hair. I had only made a few cuts when we were caught, but I had done the scalp cuts as well. Anyway, Mom cried for a while and took us to the professionals to line things out. Luckily, she said, the shag look was in, so perhaps it wasn't so horrific after all. Well, as "not horrific" as a scalp cut can be.

LET'S HEAR about my favorite Barbie of all time. She would be *sooo* not PC today. My little Barbie was Suntan Barbie, and I loved her. She wore a bikini, and under that, tan lines. Gasp! She had—*had*—long flowing blond hair. That is, until Kimberly Scissorhands came to me one day and said that she would like to cut my doll's hair like a kid at school. I guess I was imagining a cute little bob, so I went along with the idea. I couldn't wait to see my tanned little Barbie with her oh so cute new 'do. My oh so cute Barbie with her styling new 'do could have been all she could be in the army. You see, my oh so cute little Barbie with the styling new 'do, had a *burr*! Yes. She had a burr. A buzz cut. Sigh. Kim had cut her hair like a little *boy* at school who had a burr! I was crushed!

·   ·   ·

WHEN KIM and I were about ten and eleven, we got the dreaded lice. There were kids on our bus that kept it. But what we didn't understand was that there was a whole slew of them, and they were very poor. So perhaps their parents couldn't afford the treatment. (I could have loaned them our army stylist! That would have gotten rid of it!) Anyway, we had lice. The Pennington's are known for having very thick hair, and we were no exception. Would you like to know how that tiny lice comb felt going through our full, thick manes of hair? Ok, just imagine trying to gather the Japanese plant, Kudzu, with a fork. Nearly impossible!

WE HAD a friend who had less money than we did. He had to come to Kim to get his haircuts. After a few years, she got pretty good at cutting his hair. But *before* that, there were many hair mishaps. He would sit there and pray, I'm sure, for a good hair cut. But he'd usually leave our house with the same statement, "Sis, you done me bad!" He'd say that every time before pulling his hat back over his new homely 'do.

Boys are lucky. When they have bad hair, they can just sock it under a cap. We girls are not so lucky. We have to fix it the very best we can and even though we know our hair looks awful, we have to pretend that that was the intended look.

ONCE MOM WAS CURLING my hair. I liked the big banana curls, so she wound it up tight around the curling iron. The phone rang, Mom handed me the curling iron and went to step over me. She tripped over the cord and it nearly yanked my brains out with it. That was quite painful.

I HAVE ENOUGH bad perm stories to fill a novel with. Here's the problem, to get a perm professionally *installed*, it cost seventy-five dollars at the time because I had so much hair. Well, that was a lot of money. So I'd buy the six dollar home perm and hope for the best. Well, that's usually not how it worked out. I remember once I had a perm right before prom. *Big mistake!* It was rolled on the blue rollers, which are the tiny ones. I looked like an old lady with those tight curls. It was gorgeous, let me tell you! I don't think I had to get a perm for two years!

Once I let Jeannie and Nicole give me a perm. Another mistake. My hair was fried! But, had the roles been reversed, their hair would've been fried, too, because none of us knew what we were doing!

When I was a freshman in high school, I cut a picture out of a teen magazine and took it to the salon. I loved this hair do. Basically, it was Jon Bon Jovi hair that was bob length. Cybill Shepard had this hairstyle in Moonlighting. Anyway, loved it, wanted it. The chick at the Blue Bonnet said my hair wouldn't do this. Remember the old lady perm? Well, I wanted my layered bob cut and went to another shop. This lady said that the bob would look so cute on me. I knew the Blue Bonnet lady was just old and totally not hip. I was going to look oh so good.

HOLY CRAP—WHAT HAPPENED?

This was a horrible look. I can't even begin to describe it. Usually when you leave the salon, your hair is amazing, has bounce, and is full of body. Yeah? Well, I looked like an electrocuted sheep dog. The stylist wasn't even trying to sell me that "cute look" crap! There wasn't anything cute about that 'do. Just let me say that it looked so bad, in fact, that my brother called the salon and threatened them if they didn't fix my head! Now *that's* a bad haircut!

· · ·

BEFORE I NEEDED HAIR COLOR, I wanted hair color. My friend, Twynell, got a lighting mist called Summer Blond. I wanted it too. She had strawberry blond hair. I had dark brown hair. Becoming a summer blond wasn't difficult for her. Thank God my mist didn't do anything to my hair. I would have no doubt become a summer tangerine instead of blond. Why would I want to go blond, anyway? Well, since that wouldn't work, I put a pump in the peroxide. A misting pump! What was I thinking? I put a hairspray nozzle in the peroxide bottle and would spray it on my desert sand hair. It was so brittle from perming, summer blond gone awry, and teasing that it was a four alarm fire waiting to happen. But the peroxide did lighten my hair. I only sprayed it on the hair that surrounded the sides of my face. I guess I was framing that pretty thing!

ONCE I WAS FEELING down after a breakup and thought that a new shade would cheer me up. I bought the hair color, applied it, and wanted to scream. The results were exactly as the bottle promised, only that was *not* the color that I was trying to achieve. It was flaming red. The wrong bottle was in the box. I had to go to school and, once again, try to pretend that I was going for that look. I was in college by that time, so it wasn't as horrific as if it had been high school.

WHEN I WAS a sophomore or junior in high school, all my friends got their hair frosted. Well, not wanting to be different, I got a frosting kit, too. Mom and I read the instructions and went straight to work. Having your hair pulled through the tiny holes of that cap gave you insight into what childbirth would be like. That was cruel and unusual punishment. Once the torture was over with, we waited. We waited to see this gorgeous head of hair appear before our eyes.

HOLY CRAP! WHAT HAPPENED?

. . .

MY HAIR SURE WAS LIGHTER. When coloring your hair, afterthought is not a good idea. After going back and re-reading the instructions s-l-o-w-l-y, we discovered that one is not to pull *every* hair through the cap, only select strands. Highlighting. Hmm . . . there's a concept. I would have to buy hair color every so often to help reduce the glare of my oh so lighter hair.

The highlighting faze was popular with a lot of people. My uncle had a girlfriend whose hair looked like it had been lit on fire — a few times. If you knew these people, you'd know that they may have gotten desperate one Friday night and mistook it for weed. It was fried! Nonetheless, she wanted me to frost her hair, and she *did* want every strand pulled through. Well, as I performed my magic on her hair, I nearly died from secondhand smoke inhalation. I'm sure there's a warning label about that. Hey, maybe that's why her hair was so fried. Maybe it *had* ignited the time before. Anyway, I think you were to leave it on for twenty-five minutes or so. I would keep telling her it was time to rinse, and she'd say for us to leave it on a little longer. After about forty or forty-five minutes, twenty-five minutes longer than it was supposed to be on, she finally allowed me to rinse it off. If I could have hid anywhere or made myself disappear, I surely would have. Her hair was as brittle as a corn husk, and it was white as snow. I dreaded her seeing it, but I told her and told her it was time to rinse. So it was her own fault, whatever the outcome. The time had come, and she stood up to see the finished product. I winced when I heard her scream. Then I couldn't believe my ears. "I *love* it," she exclaimed. Wha? I was glad she did, but it looked terrible!

BEING that my teenage years fell in the mid-eighties, hair mishaps were inevitable. We teased, scrunched, frosted, moussed, colored, permed, gelled, and crimped our hair to death. Nothing was too big or too outrageous for an eighty's girl and her hair. We girls had to compete with the boys. It's a shame when a man's hair is nicer, longer, and bigger than yours. We did like big hair then, but some took it to the extremes. Some girls in my senior class had gigantic hair, so much so that all their hair wouldn't fit in crop of their senior pictures. My hair was big, but not *that* big. Today, I have short, straight, simple hair . . . that I like to push the volume on.

49

DADDY

MY DAD WAS A HANDSOME FELLA. HE HAD THICK BLACK HAIR, DARK SKIN, and green eyes. He had a signature look, which was black clothing from head to toe. He was a hard worker, a music lover, and a good Daddy.

MOM TELLS a story of me singing a Tanya Tucker song, Delta Dawn. It was Daddy's favorite song. I was only a year old, but I guess I was a music lover even then. She said I'd sing, "De Don," my attempt at Delta Dawn. She said it made Daddy happy that I was trying to sing.

HE DUBBED ME HIS, "POOH BABY." The nickname was shortened to "Pooh," and would stick with me until my school years.

LAST YEAR, Mom was over, and I was signing books. I had stacks laid out in front of me, along with ink pens, packaging envelopes, and a notebook to keep everything straight. I was writing an inscription when she spoke up. She said, "Your daddy would be so proud of you." It nearly made me cry. It still does.

Then she said, it used to make him so mad when people thought you were a boy! I could't help but laugh, but it sure took the conversation down a different path. One second I'm crying, the next I'm laughing.

I didn't have hair until I was at least two years old, so I guess all babies look like boys at that age.

SOMETIMES FATE DEALS A CRUEL HAND, as was the case with my dad and the accident that snuffed out his life way too soon. Today, he'd be sixty-nine years old.

He passed away when I was sixteen months old.

IN THE LAST FORTY-FIVE YEARS, he's missed his babies growing up, graduating college, giving him grand babies, and turning out to be pretty good people.

WELL, maybe he didn't miss any of these things. Maybe he's watched over us all these years, our very own Guardian Angel. Maybe he's witnessed every victory, every heartache, every misstep, and every accomplishment that we had. Maybe he didn't miss a thing. But we sure did.

50

THE LOG HOUSE AT PLUCK'S ROCK

Growing up, there was a house on Wendover that always intrigued me. Day after day, I would pass by on the bus and wonder what it looked like inside. It was a two-story wood sided house that sat just below one of my favorite bends in the road. It was cradled by a horde of native plants and trees. Just beyond that, further down the hill, was that jade green river that I loved so much. It was a picturesque Appalachian hillside, if I'd ever seen one!

I didn't know the owners and never once told anyone how badly I wanted to see inside of it.

My school days long behind me, I grew up and moved away. Time after time, when I'd go home, I'd pass by the log house. And again, I'd wonder.

Many more years passed . . .

With the invention of Facebook, I reconnected with many

acquaintances from my school days. Lots of amazing friendships were formed, most especially that of Fran Ford and Danielle Lewis. I love these girls *so* much!

In no time at all, I quickly discovered that the log house, that had piqued my curiosity for decades, *actually* belonged to them and their beautiful mother, Carol - who has also become a wonderful friend to me.

As I inquired about the home one day, I was told a delightful story about its rich and intricate history. As it was explained to me, Mary Breckinridge had a doctor named Dr. Beasley. During his home visit travels, he came to love Wendover Road and purchased riverside property from a fella named John "Pluck" Morgan. The property would go on to be named "Pluck's Rock" after the former owner and his love of fishing off the giant rock near the river.

Before this time, the Beasleys had looked at property Down the River. Mrs. Beasley had taken a keen interest in a well-constructed barn and in the stone fireplace out of the adjacent home. They purchased both. Being that the Army Corp of Engineers were set to flood the area to build Buckhorn Lake, living in that particular location was not an option. So, the barn and stone fireplace from the home were disassembled and floated on the river in route to Wendover. The log house at Pluck's Rock was erected in the early 1960s from barnwood and masonry dating back to the eighteen hundreds. Today, that stone fireplace graces the cozy family room of the log house while the corn crib and hay loft from the barn are now modern day bedrooms, an eclectic blend of two structures forming one home.

I absolutely adore convoluted history like this, and the fact that it surrounds one of my very favorite homes ever is just icing on the cake!

As often happens with close friendships, there reaches a point where you begin to feel more like family than friends. That day came, and I finally received a coveted invitation to Thanksgiving Dinner at the log house. Or maybe the first time was to Fran's wedding. At this point, I can't be sure.

What I *am* sure of is that the log house at Pluck's Rock did not disappoint!

I was giddy as a schoolgirl as I skipped down that winding path of stone steps for the first time! The house was warm and inviting as you stepped inside, filled with both modern conveniences and rustic charm.

It was everything I always knew it would be.

As lovely as the log house is on the exterior, the interior of the home itself provides a scenic view of the river that's simply breathtaking. It's one of those scenes that draws you in and makes you imagine yourself living there. Whether it be a Christmas morning filled with family and chaos, or simply the solitude of nestling in with a good book and a warm cup of hot chocolate, that flowing river just beyond the wall of windows calls to you; it anchors you; it makes you feel like coming home.

MAYBE IT'S fate that I never had the opportunity to see the log house when I was younger. I have an old soul that didn't catch up to me for many years after I left home. My level of appreciation wouldn't have been the same in those early days.

I'm a firm believer that, sometimes, you find things at exactly the right moment. When my appreciation of this magnificent rustic home could match the discovery, I think that's the moment that the universe chose to reveal it to me.

As is common in life, there are things that truly *are* meant for us; they're just not meant for us right now.

I truly believe that was the case with this home, the house at Pluck's Rock, one of my favorite bends in the road . . .

5 1

LUNCH

"Are you mad at me?"

Over the years, I've jokingly received this call many times from Bru. It always pertains to what I've packed him for lunch that day, or rather, forgot to include. Yes. I pack his lunch. No. I'm not ashamed to admit that. It's something I enjoy doing.

Anyway, many things have spurred this question. Once, I packed him chicken salad with no bread. Other times, I have forgotten to add drinks, the silverware, or something else he deemed vital.

The first time I received the distress phone call was within the first month of our marriage. Before he got in the shower one morning, I asked him what he wanted for lunch.

"Tuna," he replied.

So, I packed it up and sent him on his way.

Sometime later, I received a phone call. "Are you mad at me?"

I laughed and asked why he would think that.

Apparently, my new husband wasn't feeling the love when he opened his lunch box to find a can opener, the can of tuna, and a salt shaker. What? That's the way I ate it all the time.

We had a little discussion that night about lunchtime specifics.

Hey, it could have been worse. I used to eat Miracle Whip sandwiches. He'd had to wipe his tears with the bread had I sent that . . .

5 2

THE DRUGSTORE

EVERY SMALL TOWN HAD ONE, A BUSINESS THAT WAS PART RESTAURANT, part variety shop. For us, it was Campbell's Drug. Or as we called it, The Drugstore. Standing on the sidewalk, just beyond the Main Street of Hyden, you saw two plate glass windows that flanked either side of a swinging glass door. Pushing through the door, you stepped onto a wood floor and were greeted with a long rectangular room that was dimly lit. To the right, a tower of magazines inched up the wall. This is where I learned about Brooke Shields and her signature caterpillar eyebrows. Funny, the things we remember.

In front of the magazines were two gumball dispensers on stands. They held dozens of brightly colored little gumballs.

To the left was a long counter. Bar stools bellied up to the bar and so did the patrons who could grab a quick lunch.

The Drugstore was known for two beverages. This was the first place I ever drank a cherry Pepsi. We could get pop anywhere. But cherry Pepsi was a treat and could only be found at the drugstore. The second drink, which has become legendary to Leslie Countians, was Orangeade. This drink was similar to lemonade but made with oranges. I loved watching the ladies behind the counter make this yummy treat for us. They'd take oranges, cut them in half, and place one side—face down—on a metal juicer. They'd slide your cup under-neath then turn the handle, which lowered a metal piece that looked like an upside down funnel. It would press the orange, straining all its deliciousness into your cup, pulp and all. After a few pumps of sugar water and a generous splash of regular water, the mixture was combined. They'd sock a straw in it and off you'd go. Is this the exact way they made Orangeade? Probably not. But that's the way I remember it. What I wouldn't give to spin on a barstool while I waited for that drink . . . just one more time! But I think they'd frown upon that at my age.

When you hopped down off the barstool and walked the rest of the way into the store, a creaky wood floor would lead the way to the café tables. The only thing that stands out to me about them was the tiny metal pitchers of coffee creamer on each table.

To the left of the tables, old time cabinets spanned the distance of the back wall. They were long - about nine feet each. Ok, *maybe* that's an exaggeration. But to a little kid, they were massive. The cabinets were framed in a dark walnut. Clear glass fronts allowed a peek inside at the various medicinal remedies on display.

At the back of the store was where the pharmacist was located. I think this must've been a "no-no zone" for us, because I honestly have zero memories of this area until I was a teenager.

BACK TO THE TOUR . . .

A GIFT WRAPPING stand stood to the right of the café tables with a door to the right of that. I loved to watch the workers wrap presents. Rolls of thick fancy paper, as I called it, sat next to a tape dispenser and big bows. Even though I didn't witness it many times, I remember the presents always looking so pretty when they'd finished wrapping them. I was certain I could've made them look good, too, but never had the opportunity to try. In those days, you got spanked when you were mischievous. And if your mom wasn't available, someone else's was. Kids behaved a little better in those community "butt busting" days!

Further down the right side of the store, beyond the wrapping station, was the doodad counter. It had stuff in it, but I don't remember what. My eyes were always drawn upward and fixated on the row of guitars dangling neatly overhead. Mom always played guitar at home and in her band, so I knew exactly what an instrument could do. But a little feller couldn't reach something seventy-five feet up in the air, give or take a foot. Oh, but if I could've, I would've played myself a tune . . . Then Mom would've beat a melody onto my behind!

MOM TELLS a story of us ordering lunch one day. She said the waitress took my order. I told her I wanted a ham and cheese sandwich without the ham. She corrected that what I wanted was a cheese sandwich. Mom said I got all huffy and repeated my order. To which the waitress laughed and said, "Ok. A ham and cheese sandwich without the ham . . ."

Remember those cute little pitchers of coffee creamer? Well, my sister used to drink them . . . straight from the pitcher. She also fished gum out of the gumball machines for us, which leads me to this next thought. While she was busy doing all that and likely getting into trouble, I had plenty of time to wrap a present. Maybe two. Sigh. Missed opportunities . . .

MANY YEARS HAVE PASSED since I was last in The Drugstore. And several businesses have occupied the space since that time. What I recall are memories from when I was a kid. Are they completely accurate? Probably not. But I'm glad to have them just the same and the experience of growing up in small town USA . . .

53

CORN "FILLED" BEANS

A Hurricane Creek memory was sparked today. I was at my parents' house picking tomatoes and thought I'd check the beans while I was at it. The beans are by the corn, and that sight reminded me of a childhood misconception.

I remember hearing Mammaw talking about Cornfield Beans. I always thought she was saying corn "filled" beans—as in beans and corn in the same pod—which I thought was an incredibly interesting concept!

Of all my years of breaking beans, I never once ran across that elusive corn "filled" bean, though. And, since I thought we were all saying the same thing, I never once mentioned those dud beans. I thought we all knew they were duds.

I love when Hurricane Creek memories come out of nowhere.

5 4

THE BIG HOUSE

IN THE HEART OF APPALACHIA, HIGH ATOP A ROCKY HILLSIDE IN southeastern Kentucky, sits a picturesque two-story log cabin appropriately named The Big House - the former home of Frontier Nursing Service founder, Mary Breckinridge.

The ninety year old home features hardwood floors, exposed log beam ceilings, and vintage glass-fronted bookcases that house literature of various titles. The bedrooms are laid out much the way they were in 1925, with fireplaces gracing every space.

Modern conveniences spill over to the bathrooms which have showers that rain down delightfully strong water pressure!

I slept in the Mary Breckinridge room, the home's most requested room. The bed was exceptionally comfortable, and they even provided a selection of pillows ranging from soft to firm. It was the perfect night's sleep. So perfect, in fact, I slept through my alarm. But when I awoke, I was greeted with the wonderful aroma of bacon wafting into my room. We had a traditional mountain breakfast with bacon, sausage, eggs, biscuits, gravy, fried apples, coffee, and orange juice. A spread so delightful, it was fit for a king! Or, in my case, a good country girl.

· · ·

You may not have cell service to text or call, but you can do a quick Facebook check-in to let the world know this wonderful place exists. But, trust me, with architecture and history so rich, nature trails and a river to explore, internet connectivity will be the least of your concerns.

Michael Claussen, Development Officer at Frontier Nursing University, gave a wonderful guided tour of the house and grounds. I learned so many things about Mary Breckinridge, her mission, and the continuation of her legacy.

Whether you come for the FNS and FNU history, the solitude of a writer's retreat, or simply to experience the Appalachian culture, the Wendover Bed and Breakfast and Retreat Center - located on Wendover, Kentucky - is a place that, once you visit, you'll never forget it. And chances are, shortly after you've left - if it takes that long - you'll make plans for a return visit.

55

THE SCHOOLHOUSE

I'VE SPENT A LOT OF TIME IN A ONE-ROOM SCHOOLHOUSE, BUT NOT IN the traditional sense.

My mammaw was a schoolteacher. One of her classrooms was on Hurricane Creek in a one-room schoolhouse.

As fate would have it, she and Pappaw had the opportunity, many years later, to purchase the property where it sat.

While they had a primary residence, at some point, Mammaw turned that little schoolhouse into a home away from home.

LOOKING at the front of the schoolhouse, it was the size and shape of an old country church, minus the steeple. Single windows flanked either side of a solid white door. The exterior of the building was constructed of horizontal wood planks and painted white.

When you went inside, to the right was a small kitchen area that had been partitioned off. It was long and narrow with the sink on the left and the stove on the right. There was a small kitchen table by the window. I remember my Granny Maggard sitting there eating her Shredded Wheat. In those days, it came packaged like little bricks in wax paper pouches —three to a package. And "frosted" wasn't an option!

Back at the front door, to the left was a living room. Mammaw's furniture was covered in corduroy fabric. I can still remember the feel of the grooves against my fingertips as I dragged them across the flat armrests.

Further into the schoolhouse, a bedroom spanned the other end of the room. Mammaw had two full size beds in there that were weighted down with so many quilts, you could hardly turn over. I remember many nights when my sister, Mammaw, Granny, and I would all sleep there.

There was an upright coal burning stove to the right beyond the foot of the rightmost bed. Imagining that stove, I can almost smell the soot and see the glowing embers when the door was opened to add more coal. It kept it nice and toasty. But, should the fire go out at night, when little feet slid out of bed, the floor felt like a sheet of ice.

Even though it had been converted from a classroom into a home, the chalkboards still remained. How many kids are allowed to draw on the walls at Grandma's house and not get in trouble? We were lucky, for sure. Mammaw had pastel chalks for us to use, and we delighted in writing on those boards with them.

Even though Mammaw was just Mammaw to us, she was still a teacher at heart. We were introduced to Dick and Jane at an early age. And, of course, Spot, too. Those days in the schoolhouse were some of the happiest, carefree days of my life.

Due to an unfortunate series of events, the schoolhouse was demolished in the early eighties.

Way back when, when everyone was busy living life, no one thought to take pictures of everyday things. We automatically assumed they would be there forever. I don't have a single picture of the schoolhouse - only the one that lives on in my memories.

Maybe it's a Hurricane Creek thing that makes this place so special. But, maybe, if I've created a visual for you, just maybe you guys were able to peek inside and come along as I took a stroll down memory lane.

56

DETERMINATION OF A WRONGED WOMAN

SOMETIMES IN LIFE, YOU COME ACROSS SOMEONE WITH AN UNYIELDING will, with unwavering strength, and who's full of fight. In the mountains, we say those people are "full of piss and vinegar." And, as odd as that may sound, that's a great compliment.

MY LITTLE MAMMAW was one of those people.

TO ELABORATE FURTHER on the schoolhouse story, in the early 1980s, a coal company approached Mammaw with an idea. They proposed that if she let them transport coal across her property, she would receive great financial gains in return. They were silver-tongued charlatans who painted a picture they had no intention of delivering. In the end, they declared bankruptcy after completely stripping away any semblance of the schoolhouse and the once unmarred property that sprawled across Hurricane Creek.

I'm not sure Mammaw ever received any compensation.

. . .

BUT THAT'S only part of the story . . .

I HAVE no proof of this, but I always thought the destruction of the schoolhouse was retaliation for Mammaw not playing by the mining company's rules. They called the sheriff on her; she called the sheriff on them. They strung up "No Trespassing" signs—which she promptly *kicked* down. A power struggle ensued, and it simply went downhill from there.

BACK TO THE demise of the schoolhouse . . .

IT ALL BEGAN when the coal company knocked the schoolhouse off its footers—just over a dozen columns of stacked-stone. They claimed it was an accident. After that, they moved the building several hundred feet away, just beyond the edge of the road. When they deposited it in the new location, upon unloading it, they caused irreparable damage. The walls buckled, causing our beloved schoolhouse to nearly split in half.

I'll never forget walking up the road and seeing it. In the bottom beyond it, coal dust swirled around the vacant field that it used to occupy. The schoolhouse, which had always paralleled Hurricane Creek, now faced Preacher's Fork. Broken down, crumpled, and displaced, it was a sad reminder of all that the company had taken. As if that wasn't devastating enough, they then scooped it up, tossing it into the hole that the coal belt ran out of. It was gone forever. Those were callous acts set in motion by some very heartless men and a judge whose pockets that were lined by them.

AT SOME POINT in the process of this fiasco coming to a close, both Mammaw and the coal company had permission to be on the property at different times. Dueling court orders, I suppose. She managed to get inside the trailer, her former home and their new office, and lock them out with a padlock. She took possession of their desks, chairs, copying machines, typewriters, expensive furniture, and all their documents. They were never granted access to the trailer again.

Before the company pulled out completely, they had security guards who were tasked with escorting Mammaw off the premises, should she cross the property line. She crossed it. Repeatedly.

Even though Mammaw had been wronged, she wasn't without compassion. The guards were stationed in an uninsulated building, just feet from the trailer. A lot of the guards were people who had grown up right around Hurricane Creek, so she knew them. She didn't have ill feelings toward them. They were simply doing their jobs. And, being that she never went to jail, they weren't very good at it.

When she cooked supper, if she had extra, she'd often take a plate out to the guard—the same guard who was tasked in having her arrested. A hot meal and warm cup of coffee went a long way in persuading someone to turn a blind eye.

THERE WAS a period where everything was in limbo. Because of the court order, the company wasn't running coal. Being that they were losing money, they didn't like that and decided to forge ahead illegally with production. When Mammaw heard the belt hum to life and saw the fresh pyramid of coal start to build, she was furious! That day she decided that they wouldn't screw her out of one more dime. She grabbed her folding chair and headed down there. Granny Maggard was enraged, too. So on that evening, if you drove down Hurricane Creek, you would've seen my little Mammaw and her momma sitting in their folding chairs, in the coalfield . . . directly under the conveyor belt—which they had successfully caused to stop.

Mammaw and I talked about that day years later. I said she and Granny were very brave to take that stand but asked if she wasn't worried sitting underneath the coal belt. She just laughed and said she figured they wouldn't dump it on their heads!

WHEN THE COAL company filed bankruptcy, they not only left without paying Mammaw the monies agreed upon, but they left the land stripped, barren, and blemished. A reclamation company came in sometime later to restore the property that was mined, but Mammaw's land didn't qualify for some reason.

MY BROTHER, sister, and I were her reclamation company.

THAT FOLLOWING SUMMER, she'd roll us out of bed every morning at the crack of dawn. We'd go out into the yard and start working. We had buckets and fireplace pokers. The pokers were to unearth jagged rocks, coal, and debris. The buckets were the collection system. We walked every inch of that property over the course of the summer, Mammaw by our sides. It was a slow process, but through hard work and determination, we managed to erase the physical damage that the company caused and eventually turned those two acres back into the beautiful yards that once graced Hurricane Creek.

I WAS hesitant to include this story because coal mining already has such a black eye. It's important to remember that, in life, there are good people and there are bad. In all walks of life, races, and religions, you have a variety of people. Bad people ran this coal company. Their greedy actions - without concern for people, feelings, or possessions - resulted in the loss of the schoolhouse and the destruction of Mammaw's property. They were bad. The coal industry is not.

By the same token, not all elderly people are easy targets. Mammaw was full of piss and vinegar . . . a fact they became sorely familiar with. If they thought they could target a widow, break her, and get what they wanted, they were sadly mistaken. They backed her into a corner and couldn't handle the wildcat that emerged. She gave 'em hell, and for that, I couldn't be prouder!

57

A LITTLE BIT CATHOLIC

I WAS THINKING ABOUT THAT TIME THAT I ACCIDENTALLY BECAME ONE percent Catholic. Bru and I were at a Catholic funeral when we got separated. Everyone lined up at the end to pay their respects. We Baptists do this, too. Only, by the time I realized I wasn't in the "paying respects" line and was actually in the "communion" line, it was too late to back down. Of course, my new husband appeared just in time to give me the, "What are you doing? You're not Catholic!" look right about the time I ate my cracker. That's a look I've come to know well over the years.

58

THE CLUNKER

SOME PEOPLE DREAM OF RESTORING THEIR DAD'S 1967 MUSTANG. SOME want a little red sports car so they will look oh so cool. Others can't wait to own their first BMW so everyone will know they have finally arrived, literally and figuratively. But we just wanted a car that ran.

There's a bad part of town, every town has them. Everyone in the community knows the places to avoid. And even though we knew to avoid this place, we had to drive right through it to get where we were going. These people shot each other regularly, must have been a hobby. They shot people that they liked, so we knew they'd shoot anyone who messed with them without hesitation. The sad thing is that beerthirty arrived early for these folks, and we had a car that could make this *very* dangerous. You see, it tended to backfire without warning. And it did so one day as we were driving through this "quaint neighborhood." We were afraid that they would start shooting back because guns seemed to be as accessible to them as Benjamin Franklins are to Donald Trump! But we were lucky, and they didn't shoot us.

The old car had about all the living that it could take. It was a ginourmous 1970 something station wagon with the three rows of

seats—front row, back row, and backwards row. Now there's an ingenious plan. Pile as many people as you can into a car and then put
some of them backwards. Can you say *puke* anyone?

So d-day had come for old faithful when the new car came to
town. The "new" car was gray with orange stripes on it. Sounds
gorgeous, huh? Oh, and it cost fifty bucks. A fifty dollar car. Hmm, I
don't think when old man Ford himself rolled his first car off the
assembly line that it was as cheap as fifty dollars, so you know that
what I'm about to talk about is a gem!

The "new" car that we so jeeringly dubbed, "The Clunker" was
humiliating, to say the least. The only "shocks" on that car was had by
passersby. They were shocked that it was even in commission! This
car was unique. It had state of the art windshield wipers, an electrical
system to die for, and an engine that just wouldn't stop! HAAA. I
could hardly type all that without busting out laughing! The windshield wipers and the headlights could not be on at the same time. If
they were, the fuses would blow. It made for interesting nighttime
driving in the rain. That's not the only phenomenal part about the
wipers. If you decided that you had to have the lights and the wipers
going at the same time, you also had to elect a passenger to assist you.
It wasn't easy driving a stick shift and pulling a rope *while* driving, but
if we wanted to have headlights *and* windshield wipers, that was the
tradeoff. You see, the driver had a rope, and the passenger had a rope
—heave ho, heave ho, heave ho. The ropes were attached to the wiper
blades, and each person had to take turns pulling the wipers to the left
and then to the right to make them work. Kids today are so freakin'
spoiled!

I can hardly wait to tell you about the doors. There was a suicide
door and another suicide door, but not in the typical sense. No, I
didn't make a typo. The driver's door wouldn't open—it was welded
shut—and the passenger's side door wouldn't close. *You think I'm
joking; I know. Wish I were . . .* So, if you wanted to look really cool,
before getting out of the car, you'd roll down your driver's window
with the vice grips clipped to the roller downer because the handle

was busted off. Maybe you'd climb through the window like Bo Duke, but this car evoked enough stares and laughter on its own, so you would *never* draw that sort of attention to yourself. So instead, you'd crawl through the passenger's side door and slam a pair of blue jeans up in the door to get it to close. *You think I'm joking. Wish I were.* Actually, I have a funny story about those jeans that I'll get to later.

Once when Kim was driving the car on Hurts Creek, the gear shift came off in her hand in a steep curve. It was rather alarming, but she just jammed it back on and kept on trekking. They say in the face of adversity, you adapt and overcome. We compromised and prayed to God that we'd make it home!

This car was *full* of surprises. It would get you to a remote place and *surprise*! It wouldn't get you home without mechanical intervention. Ahhh, the memories . . . Once we drove to London to pick Nicole up. Our Aunt Carrie was pretty sure that Nicole wasn't going anywhere in *"that"* car and she told us so! After much begging, she did decide to let Nicole come back to Hyden with us. Although, she said that she wanted to change her mind when we went hopping down the driveway from lack of shocks!

KIM HAD an interesting night once when the clunker decided that it would get her where she was heading, then only get her halfway home. There was a family who used to bootleg beer, *or so I've been told.* Kim called Mom to tell her where she was broken down. When Mom asked where she was, she told her the last name of the family. This family had the same last name as the bootlegger family. Mom nearly had a stroke, but relaxed once she realized Kim wouldn't be selling beer until help arrived.

One night Kim was checking up on someone, and it must have been raining out because Nicole and I were with her. Heave ho, heave ho . . . As we snuck up the hill under the cover of darkness during operation peek-a-boo, our target came into view and was on the move. We were seconds away from being discovered. Being that there was nowhere to turn or no time, we had to head, umm . . . *back* down this huge hill—*fast!* That was a scary time. Come to think of it, a lot of the time in this car was scary! But nevertheless, the clunker did not fail us this night, and we scurried away without being detected.

Back to the jeans. Kim, Dorothy, and I went to the ice cream shop in Hyden, Don's Dairy Delight. As we sat in the car, the guy beside us, Mr. O.C.D., would not leave us alone. He continually tried to get our attention. He'd point to the door and then he would tug at his jeans. We'd signal that we knew and he'd shake his head no. When we realized that he was not gonna rest, and that we were not going to eat our ice cream in peace, we opened the door, removed the jeans, and held it shut. When we were finished eating, it was time to go. We couldn't drive with the door flopping open, so we closed the door as usual. We opened it, tossed the jean leg out and then slammed the door shut. You should have seen the look on this man's face. It was hilarious! Bless his heart, he had tried so long to get our attention so that we would take the jeans out of the door and then we put them right back. He was so confused!

Once Boose and I decided that we were gonna teach ourselves to drive. Now, there is much history behind me, Boose, and anything on wheels. So, the mere thought of us in a stick shift—two greenhorns—is very, *very* frightening! We went up the road, and I was driving. For some reason, we decided to turn around. So, we went to my Uncle Eddie's house and turned in his driveway. As we popped back out on the road, I had to stop. On an incline. No problem. I pressed the brakes casually in this clunkermobile, or maybe I pressed the clutch casually. But, apparently, I did not press them both because we shot backwards like a rocket. I kept stomping and stomping *violently* on the floorboard. Stomping with all my might. No good. We were racing toward the creek at high speed when I must have done something right, because the car finally stopped! Thank the Lord! Boose and I decided this day, perhaps, was *not* the day to learn to drive!

. . .

It's funny that the car that we *never* dreamed of having is the car that brings back so many memories! So even though it wasn't a 1967 mustang, a little red sports car, or a BMW, it was a car that ran sometimes, that got us to where we were going occasionally, and that can evoke laughter always!

59

RODE THAT HORSE LIKE A BOSS

I'm not exactly *one* with nature. Never have been. It's just not my thing. I don't like heat. I don't like most critters. And I don't like sacrificial living.

When my cousin, Boose, and I were little, we went to camp. As in sleep in a room full of strangers, take a shower in a communal bathhouse, all activities are outdoors camp. One of the activities we got (had) to do was ride a horse. She was all over it. Me? Not so much. I was kinda afraid of the horse, so I didn't want to even cross its path. They had us standing on a platform while we waited our turn to ride. When it came my turn, I decided that instead of walking down the steps, crossing in front of the horse, and then having to hoist my hind end up on it, I would just jump off the platform and land a straddle of its back. Can you picture how this ended? I'm not sure why the horse wasn't frightened beyond all belief, and why it didn't go bat crap crazy, but it wasn't and didn't. It just stood there while its rider landed, slid off the other side, and sat half posed. I had one foot on its back, the other on the ground, like some kind of dysfunctional ninja acrobat. Everyone had a real good laugh, except for me, and I had to ride that thing, anyway.

So, for anyone else who's not a fan of nature, there's no shame in admitting that the great outdoors may not be for you! You might save yourself the embarrassment later on if you put your cards on the table from the start!

60

OUR TRIBE

Years ago, Bru and I were watching TV one night - a quality legal show with police chases and perpetrators. This guy, the bad guy, mentioned something about "slapping a ho" and said he was part of the "Slap-A-Ho Tribe." We thought that was pretty funny and joked about it on and off for years. We'd make reference to belonging to the tribe, not knowing that Tyler was listening. Little ears, they're always listening!

Years later, his class was studying about Native Americans. The teacher asked the class if any of them had Native American heritage. Lots of kids shared their stories . . . including ours who proudly proclaimed that *he* belonged to the Slap-A-Ho Tribe.

When he came home and told us that he'd shared this with the class, we were mortified! Somehow, no one understood what he said.

PRAISE. THE. LORD!

We had the discussion that day that he was hillbilly and Polish and nothing else.

61

HIDING FROM THE TORNADO

EVEN THOUGH I DON'T REMEMBER MANY SEVERE STORMS IN THE HILLS of southeastern Kentucky, one storm stands out to me. It was in the late seventies, and we were under a tornado warning.

Everyone piled in at granny's house. We were all in her basement, and, I do mean *all* of us. I'm guessing there were about thirty of us - grandparents, parents, aunts, uncles, and cousins!

I remember leaning against the stone constructed support column and looking up at the shelf against the wall. Canned green beans were arranged in a straight line, along with tomatoes, corn, and pickles.

I remember thinking that at least we'd have food if we never got out.

So, to all you gardeners out there who put away food for the winter, you may be doing more than that. You may be giving peace of mind to a fretful child, stuck in a storm cellar, whose mind is causing them to jump to the worst case scenario.

62

THE HOUSE IN THE VALLEY

WHEN I WAS IN HIGH SCHOOL, ONE OF MY BEST FRIENDS LIVED IN A four-room house. It had two bedrooms, a living room, and a kitchen. There was no bathroom and no indoor plumbing. When nature called, we walked a path just beyond her house to get to the outhouse. The path itself was well-worn, but the weeds surrounding it were tall and unkempt. In the Appalachian Mountains, such conditions are breeding grounds for snakes, even though, amazingly, we never saw one.

The family's water source came from a well located along the meandering path of their driveway. A hand-cranked water pump brought the water inside and was attached to the grooved drainboard of their single basin farmhouse sink.

They did have an electric stove where her mom would boil water for dishes, laundry, cleaning, and baths. She was such a phenomenal housekeeper, it never once occurred to me that we were doing dishes where the last bath had been taken. She paired mountain wisdom along with pride in the little she had. No one ever went hungry, and no one ever went dirty.

I spent countless nights in that little house. In the winter, the home was heated by a coal burning stove in the living room. In the summer? Well, it felt about the same temperature as it did outside.

Even though they didn't have indoor plumbing, their house was always neat and tidy. There are people in the world who would use those conditions to explain away why their house was a mess. That wasn't the case with this family. Their house was always clean. Always. Before we went to bed at night, the mom would bring in a basin of water, a bar of soap, a washcloth, and a towel. We had to wash our feet just before getting into bed. Maybe it was all in my head, but I swear it made me sleep better.

The little house no longer stands in that mountain valley in Leslie County. Long gone are the evenings on the porch with the only sounds in the night air being that of the crickets, frogs, and the clackedy rockers gliding against the wood planks. The laughter is silenced now, and the stars snuffed out — at least the view I once had.

I can't say if the experiences that build us make us any better or any worse. But, one day, when we look back on our story bank of memories, experiences like those I've just described will make for more colorful stories and more heartfelt memories.

6 3

PAINT ME A PICTURE

NICHOLAS SPARKS IS ONE OF MY FAVORITE AUTHORS. MANY TIMES, when I watch a movie based on his novel, I wonder if the image I see on the screen is the portrayal he intended. He's a fascinating story-teller who causes the images to come to life, something that I admire and strive to attain myself.

When asked if I prefer movies or books, my answer is always the latter. A novel is much more in depth than a movie could ever be. If the author does their job right, the text will leap from the page, painting a picture that a digitalized image could never do justice.

When given the choice, always opt for the novel.

64

THE INTRUDER

ONE NIGHT, WE WERE LYING IN BED WHEN A LOUD THUD WOKE ME. I laid there a minute and heard it again.

AN INTRUDER . . . clearly *inside* the house.

I SAID, "BRU! Wake up! Someone's in the house!" He endured *both* shaken husband syndrome *and* hearing damage at the same time that night from his violent, shrieking wife trying to get his attention.

"Wha?" was the response I got, followed by snoring.

I cast him the evil side-eye as I grabbed a bedside baseball bat. Mad *and* scared, I stomped off into the house to take care of business.

The intruder struck again, like a little midnight ninja. I couldn't see him; but I could hear him. With my heart in my throat, I followed the sounds . . .

HE WASN'T EVEN *TRYING* to be quiet!

· · ·

WHACK.
  Pause.
  Whack.
  Pause.
  Whack . . .

THAT'S when I quickly realized that my "intruder" was no other than a helium balloon that had loosened from the doorknob, inched its way up the wall, and gotten tangled up in the ceiling fan.

  Relieved, I made my way back to bed. While I didn't wake Bru up and give him the "what for," he dang sure heard *all* about it the next morning.

THE NEXT TIME we woke up to an intruder in the night, it was a trillion times *more* terrifying because that *intruder* actually made *his* way into the bedroom — the bedroom ceiling fan, that is. Talk about a heart attack! It was no different than if you woke up to one of your kids repeatedly punching one of those giant balloons that are attached to rubber band loops. Imagine their determination to make that sucker fly. Now, imagine *that* going off right over your head when you're trying to sleep. That's what we woke up to.

FIX IT, Jesus!

65

THE CREDIT CARD

WHEN KIM AND I WERE IN COLLEGE, MOM AND CLAY GAVE US A CREDIT card - for emergency purposes *only*! Our first "emergency purchase" was a Christmas tree and ornaments. The second was Glamour Shots. Mom was not impressed with our financial reasoning nor with those things we deemed as emergencies.

NOW THAT WE'RE in our forties, I think Mom thinks we turned out to be good people. But, she's likely still concerned with our reasoning from time to time.

66

WINTER . . . 1970 SOMETHING

As the cold winds began to blow and old man winter settled in, this phenomenon would occur. Every year Mom would start saving bread bags, probably in early October. Odd, you may think. But country kids and bread bags went hand in hand in the wintertime. Or shall I say, foot and foot? You see, our loving mothers would save the bags so that we could put them over our shoes when we played in the snow. Ok, the idea was to put the bags *inside* the shoes so that our feet would stay dry. I think we kids got those wires crossed!

So off we'd go — my brother, sister, and I — into the snowy landscape. In gist, the bread bags were a really good idea. Here's the problem with wearing plastic bags *over* your shoes on wet surfaces — *they're slick!* The original plan worked great in that our feet were cozy and dry. But our butts? Well, that's another story entirely. You've seen the Three Stooges where one of the guys comes barreling into a room and meets up with a banana peel? Ok, remove the Stooge and banana peel and insert kid with plastic bread bags and snow. Result: slight concussion and bruised tail bone! And sadly, all of that occurred before we even climbed onto the sled.

We loved sleigh riding off Granny's hill for two reasons — it was a big, long hill, and the sun didn't hit it. Granny's hill was always the last place to lose the snow. There was an evergreen bush right beside her kitchen door. I loved shaking the snow-covered shrub because it would knock the snow loose, creating a blizzard. And after my concussion and sore bottom, I needed some joy in my life!

LONG BEFORE I WAS BORN, Grandpa had a lean-to shed that he kept his tools in. By the seventies, he had long since passed, but the building still remained. In the wintertime, a bunch of us kids would get up on top of the shed because the roof sloped right into the mountain, allowing us to walk right onto it. Anyway, we would get up there and lay down like little soldiers. We'd make our snowball arsenal—if we had a good packing snow—and the hunt was on. We would search out our prey and nail anyone who passed by with snowballs. That was fun for a while, but only if you were the bomber. It's no fun at all to get hit by a snowball. Let alone thirty!

I LIKED sleigh riding off Aunt Pat's hill too. Actually, it was a better hill —slope wise—than Granny's. There were two problems with this hill, however. If you made it to the bottom of the hill, you would end up right in the road, not a good thing. And there was a coal shaft that I would find every time. Maybe I found it on purpose. Because when I would land in this mini grave, my cousin, Tina, would always run to me, scoop me up, and baby me. And I liked that for some odd reason.

WINTERS WERE SNOWIER BACK in the seventies. It seemed like we always had big snows. They were so much fun to play in. Another thing that was good about a large snow was the snow cream. We took a large bowl of snow, added brown sugar, vanilla, and milk of some sort. It was good! You'd be freezing from having played outside forever, but it was a rite of passage. No matter if your bones were already chilled, you *had* to eat snow cream.

. . .

MOM WOULD ALWAYS MAKE us go visit an elderly neighbor at Christmastime and take her a gift. We would walk up the road - unsupervised, I may add. We'd walk to her house, in the snow, all bundled up because it was freezing outside. I'm sure our bread bags were close at hand . . . uh, foot. We'd arrive at her house shortly. Once we finally got her to realize who we were and convince her that we were not snow bandits, she would permit us to climb a board . . . I mean come aboard. No, actually I mean climb a board, literally because the poor thing was so scared that as protection, her porch was all boarded up. I remember her being so small. She dressed in layers, either several skirts or a long apron and skirt, multiple shirts, a house jacket, and her hair was always covered with a scarf. That's how my mind recalls it, anyway.

After climbing Mt. Saint Porch, we'd enter the inferno . . . I know that human beings were *never* meant to endure the temperatures that she lived in. Her house was the hottest place that I had ever been to in my entire life! For the walk up the road, we had on layer upon layer of clothes on, and don't forget the bread bags. By the time we had endured that walk up there, had our cardio climb, and sat down on her bed, the clothes were coming off. Then she'd start to fret because she was always afraid that we would get cold. She'd try to make us wrap up like her. Satan himself couldn't have stood the temperature of that little house - about a hundred and twenty-five degrees! That's how hot it felt, anyway. It was just awful!

She had a little dog. I don't remember his name, but I'm glad she had him to keep her company.

Before we would leave, we always went to the well to get water. She'd always say the same thing as we headed down the hill with two buckets to the well. "Run it down deep so that you get fresh water." And, as instructed, we'd run the buckets down deep.

I hated the process of going there and the smell of cleaner of some sort. I hated the intense heat, but I was always glad that we went once it was done. She was a lonely, old woman who needed company. And what did it hurt to carve out some time to go there? Absolutely nothing.

. . .

I REMEMBER GOING CHRISTMAS CAROLING. I rarely knew the words to anything other than Rudolph. So, I was always the kid who just stood in the mix, freezing my bahookie off, and just moved my mouth. While I didn't know the words, I did enjoy the spirit of Christmas and the joy we spread. When we finished singing, sometimes people would have us come in and drink hot chocolate and eat cookies or something.

THE SEVENTIES WERE SO much different from today's time. Thankfully, I still remember a time when you could be invited into someone's home, go inside, share a memory, and for that to be ok.

Sometimes going back home is simply a frame of mind, a moment in time. I'm thankful for my family, best friend cousins, and the vivid memories that I have of growing up on Hurricane Creek.

67

GRIEF

Sometimes when you're faced with a challenge, when you're writhing in feelings of despair, it doesn't feel like you'll ever push through it. But you will.

I knew I'd be sad when the time came, but nothing could have prepared me for what I felt when Mammaw passed away. I was overcome with sadness and soul crushing weeping sorrow. I'm a happy person, so to feel that despair at any given moment of the day was so odd for me.

Let me back up . . .

I remember logging on to Facebook sometime after she passed away and seeing people posting jokes and griping in general about *nothing!* I thought, "Don't they know what happened? How can they go on like nothing has changed?" Because for me, the world had crumbled.

Mammaw died on a Thursday, so every Thursday thereafter was a reminder. One week. Two weeks. Three . . . I could not move past it.

I remember saying to my friend, "Is this depression?" I sure have never been depressed before, so I honestly didn't know. Of course, it didn't affect my appetite. I still ate. But let's face it. I'm not that kind of girl! Nothing short of sewing my lips shut could affect my weight or appetite!

I finally decided that if I was sad, I would cry. I mean ugly cry. And I cried hard and often. Then it would go a day or two in between crying fits. And then a week. And then suddenly, I didn't cry at the drop of the hat anymore. And then, Thursdays came, and I wasn't sure how many weeks had passed. And then one day, I put up the wind chimes that I got at her funeral, and instead of crying when I heard them, I smiled at their beautiful melody. It made my heart happy to hear them. A reminder of her.

I wish I had documented that journey, but I didn't have my head on straight. And, I just didn't have it in me. Sometimes you won't.

Now when I think about Mammaw, if I don't dwell too long, I'm happy. I'm happy that she's no longer suffering and that she's in a better place.

WHEN YOUR HEART and mind reconcile, that brings a different sort of pain because for a moment, it seems like she's forgotten. But only for a moment. She could never be forgotten. The smile in my heart, and the memories I hold dear, assures me of that.

I share this with you as a means of having hope, should you find yourself in my situation. Whatever your soul is crying out for is what you should do. Maybe you need therapy. Maybe you need medicine. Maybe you need to cry, to scream, to hit your knees and pray, to get angry . . . and it's ok to be angry. You miss them. I miss her . . . so very much. It's all ok.

I can promise you that this raw ache won't last forever. It truly won't. And you know what? They wouldn't want it to, anyway.

MY EXPERIENCE FIVE YEARS LATER . . .

. . .

You'll have good days and bad. Expect that. Today has been one of the bad ones for me. In all honesty, I'm ugly crying right at this moment. And, that's just ok. Sometimes your memories sneak up on you . . . as does the heartache. It comes in ripples or waves. Or avalanches. Or earthquakes. Sometimes you recognize a trigger. Other times, it catches you completely off guard. Face the moments as they come. Have a snot-slingin' good cry, and let it all out. Then you can move forward. As long as you don't hurt yourself or anyone else in the process, however you handle your grief is exactly ok. There's no timeframe on the healing and no expiration date on your sadness. Remember that.

68

CEREAL

KIDS TODAY WILL NEVER KNOW THE JOYS OF DIGGING INTO THE CEREAL box—elbow deep—and fishing out the toy that was buried inside. It might not've been the best toy, but by George, it made us happy.

69

BLUE FISH

When Tyler was little, we went to the pet store and bought a fish. Now, after all the umpteen goldfish that we gave a "porcelain farewell" to, I'm not sure why I agreed to this. Nonetheless, I did, and that little fella needed a name. He was a feisty little beta fish with graduated shades of color spanning from his navy blue body to his electric blue tail fins. Faint hues of crimson were sprinkled throughout his frayed fins. Since his color wheel was predominantly in the cobalt family, Tyler named him, "Blue Fish."

In years past, back in the goldfish days, those little fellas had unique names, too. Tyler had three friends whose names were Tate, Trevor, and Micah. At one point, after a fall festival at church, my sweet boy had won three goldfish. He named them Tyler, Tate, and Trevor-Micah. Bless it!

Anyway, beta fish typically live three to five years with proper care. Being that we'd said goodbye to roughly twenty-seven goldfish prior to Blue Fish's arrival, "proper care" was something that obviously wasn't my strong suit.

People used to say, "Aren't fish so relaxing to watch?"

I had a standard reply. I'd say, "No, because they're always floating belly up at the top!"

Blue Fish, on the other hand, did some living! He graduated from his little fish cup to a bigger aquarium that was decked out with a light, colorful rocks, plastic trees, and a little multi-level fish cave. It was a pretty sweet setup. He hung with us for years and years.

When Tyler was in kindergarten, they had pet day. At the time, we had a cat and a fish. I loaded them up and took them both to school. In hindsight, that was terrible thinking. Lexie, the cat, probably thought I'd packed her a tasty little blue treat for the road!

Blue Fish survived Show and Tell and continued to live in little fishy nirvana many more years. Alas, his day in the sun came to an end.

Even though we'd lost a ton of fish before, this one was the family pet. Even I was sad. Not that I'm Satan, but experience has taught me not to get attached to Fish 1, Fish 2, Tate Fish, Trevor-Micah Fish, "Fish that died before we got it out of the bag" fish, Bob . . .

This time was different. It was a terribly sad day at the Brudnicki house. I called Bru and gave him the news of Blue Fish's passing. We discussed how we would proceed. As responsible parents, we did the only thing we could. I took Tyler into the playroom, sat him down, and asked what game he wanted to play. What else was I to do while Bru was at the pet store buying a replacement fish, you know, one that looked *identical* to Blue Fish? *No way* was I gonna break my baby's heart! We'd save that honesty crap for another day.

I heard Bru in the kitchen rustling around. Operation Switcheroo was complete. Tyler and I came out of the playroom and went to say hi to his daddy who had "just got home from work." It *was* a work of sorts. "Blue Fish" was happily swimming around his new home. And since we needed food, his new food was plopped down on the counter right beside his fancy, sparkling clean condo. I stared in horror. Our plan had gone terribly awry. And Tyler had just taken notice . . .

"Mommy, Daddy, Blue Fish is turning *red*!" He paused in confusion. "And he's so small!"

In that moment, I did the only thing a good mommy would do. I told a bold face lie. "It's the new food, baby. It's bringing out the red in his fins."

We all have our own parenting styles. Ours were based on lies and deceit. Don't judge!

Back to the story . . . Blue Fish's new food, and its magical abilities, had that child highly inquisitive. We finally told him the truth. "Blue Fish" became "Sharkey." And, to be honest, I have no memory of Sharkey beyond that day. RIP, Sharkey. I assume you're dead.

HERE'S the moral to this story: Beta fish really do have the potential to live five years or more. And, sometimes, it's ok to tell little *red* lies . . .

70

MY UNCLE

Bru and I were at the store when I saw my Uncle Eddie shopping. We were in a hurry, so I was just gonna scoot down the aisle *real quick* to say hello. I said, "How are you?" as I grabbed him by the shoulders and spun him around to pull him into a hug.

That man was not my uncle!

I think we were kin, though, because when I spun him around, I'm fairly certain my "OMG!" expression looked exactly like the "OMG!" expression he had!

I said, "You're not my uncle!" I patted him on the shoulder and took off!

I don't think he uttered a single word during that encounter, unlike my husband who can't stop teasing me about it to this day!

71

CHRISTINE

WHEN I SET MY MIND TO DO SOMETHING, I'M PRETTY STUBBORN, AND don't stop 'till it's done. That being said, Christine and I mowed grass this evening. "Who's Christine?" you may ask. Well, that's what I've renamed my lawnmower after she tried to kill me tonight.

First of all, the mower blade lowered without my assistance—or, without me realizing I had assisted. I shrugged my shoulders and carried on about my business. Christine had to die a few times, something she never does. *Then*, she and I mowed grass at about a hundred miles per hour. Did I mention that Christine is a *push mower*? So, yeah, we mowed grass running, something I've never done before! Ever try to start a push mower, running? It's interesting; I promise you. There was no backing up if I missed a spot. She had two speeds: off and one hundred miles per hour forward. No in between. The fence line was a little hard to maneuver at that speed, but I adjusted, rode that horse like a boss, and we plowed on. The good news is that I mowed the back yard in about 2.7 minutes flat.

In true "Christine" fashion, when Bru came home, she straightened her bipolar self *right* up, as if nothing was amiss. He walked out on the porch. I squeaked out a barely audible, "Hi," heart pounding, lips sticking to my teeth, and looking like I'd been through something!

You know how in cartoons when people are scared and take off running, busting right through the wall, leaving only a body shape in their wake? Well, if you all see a push mower driving itself through the neighborhood, you'll know that Christine has roared to life in the middle of night and busted out of the storage building!

7 2

BURNIN' 'EM DOWN

MUCH LIKE MYSELF, TYLER NEVER WAS A MORNING PERSON. I'D WAKE him up for school, and the grumbling would start.

"I hate school," he'd fire off as he stomped off to the shower. "School is *stoooopid,*" he'd scream as he yanked the shower curtain back to climb in. "I hate stupid school! I hate the person that invented school! I wish they'd *all* burn down . . ."

Bru would call every morning after he got to work. "How's he doing?" He'd ask.

"Burnin' 'em down!" I'd reply.

This same scenario repeated every morning. Tyler would go into the shower a school hatin' pyromaniac demon. But, when he came out, he was like a different child. He was pleasant, and happy, and his criminal mind and blackened heart had softened to something more in line with what a five year old should have. Yes, my sweet baby just needed time to wake up.

HE GETS that from his momma.

7 3

FANCY WRAPPING

WHEN I WAS LITTLE, I USED TO WRAP GIFTS FOR MOM AND GIVE THEM to her all through the month of December. They were always things I'd found lying around the house—a stack of coins, a handful of nuts, Bub's baseball cards, one of her house shoes, probably a fork . . . The selection differed daily. What never varied was my gift wrap—black electrical tape.

Every. Single. Time.

I'd wind it on until not a single bit of the item showed through. My gifts were peek proof and nearly un-openable. But, highly anticipated, I. Am. Sure.

This technique didn't stop at Christmastime, either. Kim was in the hospital once when she was little. I picked out a Strawberry Short-cake doll at Maloney's to make her feel better. (Needed one for myself, too!) When Mom took it to her in the hospital, it was wrapped up fancy. You guessed it, in black electrical tape.

TODAY, thirty-five years later, I took a gift over to Mom and Clay's house. You better believe that I wrapped it up in electrical tape. I had fun recreating the memory.

74

MEMORY LANE

You can't find Memory Lane on the GPS, but I'd wager a bet that it's the most sought after destination that this great big ole world has to offer.

75

MAMMAW'S PEACH COBBLER RECIPE

29OZ CAN SLICED PEACHES
   ½ stick butter
   1 cup flour
   1 cup milk
   1 cup sugar
   Additional cinnamon and sugar to top
   350°
   18 minutes

POUR SLICED peaches with heavy syrup into 13 x 9 glass pan. Cut each slice into thirds. Warm peaches in microwave. In a separate bowl, mix flour and sugar. Warm milk. Add to flour mixture. Add melted butter. Once combined, pour over peaches. Stir lightly to mix throughout.

BAKE 10 MINUTES. A light crust will have formed by now. Remove casserole dish from oven. Sprinkle cinnamon and sugar on top of cobbler—in country terms, 'till it looks right! Return to oven eight more minutes. Broil till desired color is achieved. Or, in country terms, 'till it looks right!

Enjoy!

76

CUSS WORDS

I SAID MY FIRST CUSS WORD ON A DIRT ROAD—SON OF A GUN. I MIGHT'VE been seven years old. I was cussing the bus driver who made us walk home from Wendover. It seemed every bit of fifteen miles to my little legs.

IT MIGHT'VE BEEN one mile . . . uphill, both ways.

I OBVIOUSLY HAD an aversion to exercise even back then! Son of a gun, that's rough talk. I was mad. My cousin, Amy Maggard, didn't bat an eye at my trash talking. Now, I know why. It wasn't actually a bad word. But, in my mind, I'd given that man down the road—that's country speak for talked real bad!

77

PRE-LIT CHRISTMAS TREE

FOUR YEARS AGO, I SUCCUMBED TO THE FRUSTRATION KNOWN AS "Tangled Christmas Lights." I was fed up and had had enough. I tossed my beautiful Christmas tree onto the curb and headed out for a new one. It was gonna be awesome.

And, it was, the first year. Here's a poem I wrote the second time we put the tree up.

BRUDNICKI CHRISTMAS POEM, 2011

OH, Christmas tree, Oh, Christmas tree,
    You really are a pain to me.
    Oh, Christmas tree, Oh, Christmas tree,
    Why can't you lighteth the way you used to be?

OH, Christmas tree, Oh, Christmas tree,
    Everyone's making fun of me.

Oh, Christmas tree, Oh, Christmas tree,
I really wish you had been free . . .

78

JAILBIRDS

WHEN MY BROTHER, SISTER, AND I WERE LITTLE, MOM TOLD US IF WE ever went to jail that they'd feed us muddy water and stale bread. Now, we Pennington kids knew good food when it was presented to us and knew a bad idea when we heard one.

THIS MEAL PLAN, I am sure, is the driving force as to why I've never been to jail.

7 9

ELECTION DAY

ON ELECTION DAY, I'M ALWAYS REMINDED OF MY LIFELONG BEST friend, Audrey L. Clowers, and our televised political debut.

When we were young, maybe ten years old, our cousin ran for County Judge Executive of our hometown. We were at his rally handing out buttons and walking around with signs. They may have been poster boards, but I swear, my mind recalls the ones that go over your shoulders so you can advertise from the front *and* the back. That could be memory lane exaggeration, though.

Anyway, the news crew showed up, which piqued our interest greatly. We walked past them, again and again. And, again until they finally spoke to us. They asked us if we wanted to be on camera. Did we ever!

Talking was our thing! Until it was time to do it . . .

The cameraman grabbed his camera, pointed it at us, gave us the cue, then we froze. He cued us again.

You know those inclement weather eyewitnesses that always spot the tornadoes and rising flood waters? Well, we were the kid versions of them.

After the deer in the headlights blank stares, we dissolved into a round of high pitched giggles. Then, with a country accent that Honey Boo Boo would've be proud of, we plugged our candidate. "Vote for Earl Fields!" Then we giggled some more.

And, just like that, we were stars!

WELL, that may also be memory lane exaggeration . . .

80

HALLOWEEN COSTUMES OF THE SEVENTIES

HALLOWEEN COSTUMES, THEY'VE EVOLVED OVER THE YEARS. AT ONE time, you could grab a ratty sheet from the linen closet, cut eyeholes in it, sock it over your head, call yourself a ghost, and head out on a candy seeking mission.

TODAY'S COSTUMES are much more elaborate.

I WISH I had thought to ask my Mammaw how they dressed up for Halloween or if they even observed it. I remember her mentioning "false faces," but did she mean face paint or masks?

KIDS TODAY HAVE PLUSH, furry costumes that, at one time, you only ever saw in the movies. The ones we had when I was growing up were much more generic. Not that that's a bad thing. We sure thought they were fantastic! They were packaged in square boxes with the mask showing through the clear plastic front.

. . .

YOU HAD tiny pinholes to see out of and not much bigger ones to breathe out of. They sure made a Pennington child sweat! If you weren't gentle with them, the thin rubber band that secured the mask to your head would snap, causing a horrific sting to your fingers and face! And, if you were of any size at all, the rear end busted out of the costume. It wasn't funky being chunky!

I CAN STILL REMEMBER the sound of the squeaky costumes and the smell of the vinyl . . . takes me straight back to The Dime Store - 1970 something . . .

81

AFTER THANKSGIVING

My husband and I have an ongoing battle of wills when it comes to putting up the Christmas tree. I think mid-November is a great time. He counters that it should be after Thanksgiving.

Here's an actual conversation we had about that.

"I don't know why you won't let me put up the tree!"

"I will . . . after Thanksgiving."

"I'm a grown woman. I don't know why I'm asking your permission, anyway! I could march right up in that attic and get the tree. But, do me a favor. If it knocks me back down the steps and pins me to the floor, take mercy and get it off me."

"I will . . . *after* Thanksgiving."

He has come around over the years and is receptive to putting the tree up whenever I mention it. Halloween night seems like a good goal this year. Just to see his reaction . . .

8 2

THE RACE CAR TRACKS

I GREW UP IN A TIME WHEN PEOPLE SPANKED THEIR KIDS. THIS WAS AN acceptable practice, and we never thought anything of it. It was the 1970s and eighties.

I'm not sure why every parent on the creek had purchased race car tracks for their kids that year, but it seemed that they dang sure had. My memory recalls white, flexible plastic race car tracks with red and blue road stripes on them. Those were the ones we had. Our cousins may have had different ones. Heck, *we* may have had different ones. But those were the ones that come to mind.

Even though the majority of us who played together were girls, Bub had a great say in the games we played and in the style that we played them. We were tomboys to the hilt. None of us were girly girls, and I do mean none of us. They didn't buy us dresses too often because I'm sure we would've climbed a tree in 'em. I can't stress firmly enough that we were tomboys through and through.

So, when I say that we had race car tracks, it's because we all did. We enjoyed playing with cars just like the boys did.

At some point, our love for those race car tracks faded because our parents discovered that they made excellent spanking tools. Now, they didn't have Google, YouTube, Pinterest, Facebook, Wikipedia, texting, or even a flippin' carrier pigeon! But, somehow, they all seemed to discover it, relay it, and administer it *all* at the same time.

WE CALLED A COUSIN MEETING, and the plan was formed.

EVERYONE DISPERSED TO THEIR HOMES, gathered their race car tracks as covertly as possible, and met back at our house—the ones who could, anyway. We pretty much had free rein to roam the holler. Well, that's an exaggeration. Our parents always thought we were at someone else's house. To us, *that* was free rein to roam the mountains, creeks, pick some berries, and inch just beyond our boundaries to visit a coal mine or feed a horse. Free rein holler children. Free rein-*ish*.

BUT, I digress . . .

So, the cousins would meet back at our house, race car tracks in tow. We had an area of the yard, down by the creek, where we had a burn pile. We would meet down there. And, as if placing our offerings at the temple, we would place our race car tracks on the fire. As we'd watch that plastic curl, turn inward, and shrivel into nothingness, we smiled knowing that another spanking tool had bit the dust.

ANOTHER ONE BITES THE DUST . . .

83

THE WATERSLIDE

WHEN TYLER WAS LITTLE, WE WANTED TO GIVE HIM AN EXTRA SPECIAL treat, so we bought him a fifteen foot tall, inflatable water slide from Walmart - the ones with steps up the side and a small pool at the bottom.

Being that I wanted to have some summertime fun, too, I pulled myself up those stairs, near death after only one trip. I knew I exceeded the weight limit but threw caution to the wind—we all know they just make up those restrictions, anyway. Right?

Well, I started down the slide, and it was fun. I gained momentum. Too much momentum. I thought, "STOP, momentum! Just stop!" But, it didn't listen. I hit that pool and kept right on going over the end, water spilling out like the great flood, me careening through the air like Speed Racer. I stopped just shy of the storage building. JUST. SHY.

Annnnnd, that, children, is why we have a one story, no frills kiddie pool to this day. And, why I probably should walk with a limp.

8 4

MUSIC

I LOVE MUSIC. I ALWAYS HAVE. SOMETIMES IT SPEAKS TO WHERE I AM IN
life, sometimes it lends a voice to the things I can't, and sometimes it
provides a glimpse to where I'm going. I love its ability to always
express the emotion that I feel in my heart, even if those words have
failed to form.

85

THE RAZOR

WHEN I WAS PREGNANT WITH TYLER, WE WENT TO MY IN-LAW'S HOUSE
for a visit. They had a shower without a seat, which made shaving my
legs difficult. My big ol' baby bump made it hard to bend over in the
shower without toppling over. My mother-in-law had an electric
razor she said I could use. I know that it's gross to use someone else's
razor, but desperate times call for desperate measures.

I had only just begun to use it when the battery started to die. It
didn't matter anyway since it gave a pretty pitiful shave to begin with.
Nevertheless, I used it until the charge was completely gone, then
looked around for the cord so I could continue. When I found it, I
thought that it was strange that it was a different color than the razor.
However, it fit like a glove, so I had no hesitation plugging that kinky,
curly cord into the wall.

I sat on the edge of the bed and propped my foot against the wall. I
switched the power on and resumed shaving. Now, the sequence of
events that followed are a little dicey. I don't recall why I threw the
razor. I don't know if it got hot, shocked me, made a buzzing sound,
or what. I mean, *all* those things happened. I'm just not sure what
happened first. Anyway, I dropped it and screamed when it made a
popping sound.

My mother-in-law heard the shriek and came to the door. She asked me if I was ok.

"I'm fine," I squeaked out, perhaps a little too eagerly. You see, how was I going to tell her that I was in the process of burning down her house? The room was quickly filling with smoke.

Despite my claims, she barged through the door, anyway. She fanned her hand in front of her face. "Oh, my!" she said. "Let's open this backdoor."

When the smoke cleared, I saw the razor halfway across the room, along with a nearly straight cord. *Apparently*, the plug I used to charge the razor went to a different device. How was I to know? It fit. It might've walked like a duck and talked like a duck. But it *damn* sure wasn't a duck!

My husband tried to explain the whole AC/DC thing to me. I didn't know what the heck he was saying and still don't. The only AC/DC I was familiar with was the classic rock group. And "Thunderstruck" seemed to fit this moment perfectly fine.

Since that day, I have always made sure the colors match when pairing a cord with its device. And, to this day, I still get nervous if I plug something in that I had to search for the cord . . .

86

BIRTHING BABIES

In 2010, my great nephew was born. I came prepared for the long haul, snacks and Sudoku book in hand. I know what you're thinking, and I can't believe I ate in front of her, either!

The windowsill of the birthing room served as my staging area, holding my drink, donuts, and puzzle/recording vitals/whatever else they said, book. I had just taken a bite of donut when the doctor came in for a little glance. Just real quick. I wanted to be attentive, so I moved across the room and took a seat beside Tosha's mom, Vickie.

The doctor plopped down on the little rolly stool, inched closer to Natosha, fished around a second, then told her to push!

Push? Wha?

I wasn't "pushin'" company, and neither was Vickie. We were just the pre-show/after party gang. We all thought she was just "practicing" for the big moment. You know, once she understood *how* to push, *then* we'd leave, *then* she'd have a baby. Just them. She and Davis, like they had hoped.

Well, no, that's not how it went down. When the doctor told her to push, we ALL had that, "Oh, crap!" look on our faces. Well, everyone but the doctor, whose only focus was on delivering a baby.

The new parents-to-be said we could stay, so we did. Time went on, and Tosha was in a great deal of pain, which was hard to watch. Once the epidural kicked in, she was a happy lady again. When she was no longer in distress, a collision course of thoughts raced through my mind: I hoped she'd have an easy delivery. I wondered what he'd look like. I knew she'd be a terrific mother . . .

AND, at what point was it acceptable to go finish my donuts?

87

GROW WHERE YOU'RE PLANTED

As I was driving today, I saw a pink tulip. It stood tall and beautiful at a vacant home among a yard full of weeds and unkempt grass. It made me realize some things: You can find the beauty in most anything if you take the time to discover it. Regardless of your situation, you are not defined by the circumstances that surround you. It's ok to be different. Sometimes being different is the very thing that makes you beautiful. Be your own kind of beautiful.

88

THE OLD WEATHERED CHAIRS

SOMETIMES YOU RUN ACROSS SOMETHING AND JUST KNOW THERE'S A story in it. That was the case recently when I found a pair of old wooden chairs at Mom and Clay's house. They were folding chairs with weathered wooden planks. With the seats being so narrow, I didn't dare set in them for fear of having a Goldilocks' moment. The only weight they bore was the scrutiny of my stare as I imagined their history.

Some people might look at them and see a couple of old junky chairs, while others would see potential profit from an uncovered antique. But, when I run across things like those, I see a story—an untold story. I imagine the church services the chairs have seen, the family reunions, the funerals, the graveyard clean offs, the weddings, two friends catching up, or cooling down . . . I imagine the conversations that took place there and the decisions that were made. I picture squirmy little youngins' dreaming up mischief. Being that I'm a fan of shenanigans, I like those imagined kiddos very much.

Everyone and everything has a story to tell if you choose to look deeper. I guess I just always choose to look deeper. And, that's ok.

8 9

FLACKEY SCHOOLHOUSE

ONE OF MAMMAW'S FIRST TEACHING JOBS WAS IN A ONE-ROOM schoolhouse on Flackey, a holler in Leslie County. Throughout the years, she'd tell us stories about Flackey School, about riding a mule to get there, and about her time teaching—how she'd teach a year and save her money for college tuition. Then, she'd go to college a year. She repeated this process until she got her degree.

A COUPLE YEARS AGO, I thought about some of those stories Mammaw told and went back to that holler to see if the one-room schoolhouse, with its coal-burning stove and vintage piano, was still there. Kim and I found it. And it was heartbreaking. The schoolhouse that Mammaw had spoken so fondly of had toppled over, its collapsed ruins sprawled out across the schoolyard.

I COULDN'T HELP but wonder why no one preserved it—someone like a historical society—why they couldn't see the importance. It made me sad.

. . .

So, I did the only thing I could think to do. I found the property owner and asked permission to take a few planks. As it turns out, Mammaw was *her* school teacher. That nearly made me cry. With her permission, I drove back to the site of the schoolhouse and gathered some wood. My intended purpose was to write a story—a one-page story—and use the wood from the building to frame it.

And if I ever manage to condense the story to one page, I'll do just that. Or maybe my frame will be just as long as the following story . . .

Flackey Schoolhouse

Some look at this and only see a board. But this board, just like people, is so much more. This old plank came from the Flackey school, which was a one-room schoolhouse that my little Mammaw taught in. It was also a church at one time. So over the years, these walls have bore witness to lost souls, saved souls, and old souls like me. Like anything in life, if you choose to look past the imperfections, you'll see the good in something, or in people, every single time.

I guess we could call this the board of education.

When I think about this one plank, I think about the stories it could tell. I think about the times that my little Mammaw walked passed it, and maybe her skirt tail skimmed the board. I think about the children in the classroom and all those whispered secrets that no one heard. I think about people coming into the building to worship—the prayers, the joy, the sorrow, the happiness.

If I close my eyes, I imagine the children in another era. I imagine the clothing that they wore, the lunches they packed, and the games they played. Maybe they rested their little arms against the wall—this board—with their heads pressed against it, shielding their eyes in a game of hide-n-seek. Maybe they gazed against this board and dreamt of the home they'd have one day. Or maybe they gazed at this plank and dreamt up a tall tale to get them out of trouble with their momma.

THIS ONE PLANK has bore witness to teachers showing up early on horseback for the school day, to the late-night lesson planning, to students rushing into the building—whether they wanted to be there or not, to after school escapades, to Sunday School, to Bible School, and then to the day when the walls finally buckled and crumbled, bringing an end to an era that was spectacular in so many ways . . .

WHEN I LOOK BACK on the *teenage me*—or even the *me* that I was when I was twenty years old—and I think about the *me then* seeing the person that I am now talking about a board, I'm pretty sure I would've said, "Good Lord, woman! It's just a board." Sometimes it takes a while for your old soul to catch up with you, and I'm mighty thankful that mine finally has.

I'M JUST MORE aware of stories these days, most especially those that are only memories now. Everyone and everything has a story — including this old board of education, circa early nineteen hundred . . .

90

LIGHT BREAD

One night, Bru and I were discussing sandwiches. Sometimes my raising slips out, and I use words and phrases that he wasn't accustomed to hearing in Chicago.

Apparently, from his look of confusion, they don't say "light bread" in the big city. I explained that light bread is just another word for white bread, which he wondered why I didn't say that in the first place.

Even after twenty years, I still manage to shock him with my vernacular.

91

GETTING HEALTHY

I READ THAT PECANS WERE HEALTHY. SO I HAD MYSELF A BOWL OF butter pecan ice cream. This living healthy may be easier than I thought.

92

KINDERGARTEN GRADUATION

AT THE END OF MY KINDERGARTEN YEAR, WE WERE GEARING UP FOR graduation. We didn't have the fancy caps and gowns that they have now. But we were able to make our own caps, so that was pretty exciting.

We used construction paper. One piece was cut in half, lengthwise, then glued into a circle to custom fit our noggins. Another piece was laid flat, then it was glued on top of it. Miss Howard wrote, "Kindergarten," with glue, and then we were allowed to sprinkle red glitter over it. And, just like that, a fancy little hat was made.

During graduation practice, they'd coach us on standing in a straight line and being quiet. They told us how proud our parents would be when they saw us march.

ON THE DAY OF GRADUATION, I wore a little white dress that came a few inches above my knees, frilly white socks, and black patent leather shoes. Somehow, I was in the front of the line—which was odd. My last name began with a "P," and, I was one of the tallest kids in the class. I don't know. Maybe they went in alphabetical order by first names. Whatever the reason, I was line leader.

. . .

AND, they were 'bout to get a show!

THEY WALKED us to the gym door, and *I* took it from there. Remember how they told us to march and that our parents were gonna be so proud? Well, by golly, march I did. I could've put a soldier to shame. I placed my hands on my hips and led my platoon straight to our assigned location.

I don't know how "proud" my mom was. But, I know she, and everyone else in attendance at the old Hyden gym, was entertained that day that I graduated kindergarten like a boss!

9 3

CHEWING TOBACCO

WHEN I WAS LITTLE, MY UNCLE RALPH WOULD COME DOWN OUT OF HIS holler, Ralph's Branch, to visit us from time to time. We were standing on the porch one day just looking up at the road, because that's what you do in the country — you just stare at things, sometimes. He pulled his pouch of tobacco out of his pocket, along with his knife. The tobacco was pressed into a brick-like shape. He cut off a little plug, just enough to chew. I watched with a curious eye as he did this and told him I wanted to try some, too. He assured me that I would not like it. But it looked so good that I just knew he was mistaken. I convinced him to give me some. It was going to be awesome.

Imagine taking a big bite of pepper, grass, dirt, and fire. Well, that's what that delightful looking plug of tobacco tasted like. Earthy awful-ness! I hated it, of course, and I spit and spit! And spit. It was the nastiest thing ever!

As quickly as chewing tobacco had been added to my "things I must try" list, it was crossed off equally as fast!

MY FIRST POEM

ABCDEFG,
  If I love you,
  Then you love me.

I WAS in the second grade, and he was in eighth. He surely did not love me, or my poem.

I mean, seriously. How can you not love *that*?

95

NAP TIME

WHEN I WAS AROUND THREE YEARS OLD, WHEN WE WERE AT MAMMAW'S, we had nap time whether we wanted it or not. Well, being that I was a kid full of energy, I didn't want it!

She had a king size bed that she, Kim, and I would all pile in and take the forced nap. Mammaw, being a hard working granny, needed a nap. Even though Kim didn't complain, I didn't need one, and wasn't going to take one! I always had to sleep in the middle.

I waited until I was sure everyone was asleep. I had things to do and a house to plunder through. Unsupervised was the prime time to do it! I'd take that journey down those fifteen pounds of covers and work and work until I busted loose.

I had to go out the bottom because Kim and Mammaw were asleep, and if I crawled over them, they would've woken up. But Mammaw always tucked the bottom cover as if she were passing a military inspection, so I had to kick a little to bust free. As soon as my feet were on the floor and sweet freedom was about to be mine, Mammaw would say, "Now you can crawl right back up here, and get in this bed!" I would object profusely on my way back up, but always fell asleep. I was always the last to wake up.

But, I didn't need a nap . . .

96

MY FIRST LOVE

I FOUND MY FIRST LOVE WHEN I WAS A MERE SIX OR SEVEN YEARS OLD. He was quite a bit older than me. In fact, he drove a car and drank beer at the local tavern called the Boar's Nest. But, it was love. I saw him once a week, and I was mesmerized. I think he must have been poor though, because he wore the same thing nearly every time that I laid eyes on him. He had a yellow button-down shirt, faded jeans, and cowboy boots. He had blonde wavy hair. He was something. He was Bo from the Dukes of Hazzard, and he was mine!

Once, I was on a play date. In those days, we just called it playing, though. My friend and I were gonna call our boyfriends. Now, you just remember that Bo was mine—all mine. Well, that little girl got on the play phone first, and who do you think she called? Of all the boys in the world—real and imagined—she chose *my* boyfriend.

She didn't see it coming, really. She said, "Is Bo there?" And, I nearly died. Well, after a heated round of words, the fight was on. We were yelling, screaming, pulling hair, and rolling around her bedroom floor like a couple of wrestling divas!

I don't recall who won the fight, but I can tell you who won the boy. Well, neither of us. And, we're not speaking to this day . . .

97

UNSOUGHT ADVICE

HERE'S SOME ADVICE THAT I PASSED ALONG TO A FRIEND WHEN HE WAS dealing with his dad's dementia. This is some wisdom I wish someone would have given me. The truth is, when you're dealing with situations for the first time, you don't know which questions to ask; you don't know what you wish you knew.

This, of course, is based on my own experiences as a family member. My hope is that it will help someone who reads it. The night I posted this to my friend's Facebook page, I had people comment and message me. They thanked me. One lady said that she had tears streaming down her face over the truths I wrote about.

HERE'S MY MESSAGE:

"When dealing with dementia/Alzheimers, the truth is that this comes in stages. And, sadly, stress accompanies nearly all of them. You have done everything you could do to keep your daddy home. When that became an issue, you moved him in with you and your wife. There's a lot to be said about the woman she is because not everyone would have agreed to it. Dementia / Alzheimer's is a cruel disease for the entire family. There's a lot to be said about the man you are for such selfless act, too. Not everyone would or could do that. But, y'all did.

If your dad had surgery recently, and seems like he did, anesthesia is devastating to someone with dementia/Alzheimer's disease. It often erases or momentarily diminishes their abilities. The progression afterward is heartbreaking. Sometimes they actually do break free from those chains and bounce back. My little Mammaw did. Until the next surgery, that is.

One of the hardest decisions a family will ever have to make is to put a loved one in a nursing home. The stress and self-doubt that accompanies that decision is unlike any other.

It's heartbreaking.

But, you do it because it is your final hope at keeping your dad safe and properly cared for. That's what it comes down to. It's not about shipping them off at the first possible moment so you can set back at home with your feet kicked up! It's not about that at all. You do more worrying when they are away from you than you ever did when they were in the next room. You feel like a failure. Or, at least, I did. And, that amplifies that heartache.

After some time, it does get easier. That in itself brings its own level of stress.

I know you are a man, but you need to remember you are human. When you feel like crying, you cry. It's ok. That is your body's way of relieving stress. It's not a show of weakness. It's a show of how deeply you care.

Visit every opportunity you get. Call and check on him when you can't.

When you visit him, let him be whoever he is that day, in that moment. Often times, things that agitate them will be quickly forgotten if you let it. Don't try to make him remember. Just be. If he likes certain songs, sing them to him—even if you can't sing. He could use the laugh. Share stories that you know he loved. But don't press him for details. He'll provide them if he can. And, even if they're wrong, that's ok, too.

Sometimes they don't recognize you. Take that opportunity to meet a new friend. Just let him be who he is every single day in any given moment. And sometimes he'll say he's younger than you. And he believes it. Don't challenge that, or else you'll get a fat lip!

Sometimes they'll ask about a relative. And sometimes that relative has been dead for thirty years. Don't tell him that. Just say, "I haven't seen him today." No sense traumatizing him twice.

I'm praying for you and your family, friend. The weight will lift, I promise. It won't disappear, but it will get easier."

9 8

FANCY EATIN'

WHEN WE WERE LITTLE, MAMMAW WOULD TAKE US TO CHURCH. LIKE many families, once church was over, we'd go somewhere to eat.

Now, being that Hyden was a small town, we didn't have the plethora of choices that larger communities have. At the time, we had very few sit-down restaurants and only one fast food joint.

Don't you worry, though. We ate. We certainly did. Mammaw carted us right down to the hospital cafeteria where we'd fill our plates then fall in line, single file, so we could wait our turn to be checked out by the cashier.

It wasn't until later in life that I found this to be unusual.

99

SLAMMIN' DOORS

WHEN TYLER WAS LITTLE, WE HAD AN EXCEPTIONALLY TRYING DAY ONE day. For some reason, he was upset with me and expressed that by slamming his bedroom door—repeatedly—to prove his point.

Time after time, he'd go in and out of his room, slamming the door so hard he nearly splintered it. Ok, that's a *slight* exaggeration.

But he'd give it heck as his angry little self crashed it together time and time again.

THAT DAY, my mood seemed to match his because on one of the final window-rattling whams, I headed for the junk drawer.

IN JUST A SPLIT SECOND, I jerked that door open and lurched inside the bedroom.

Tyler was still mad, so the devil in his eyes matched the one in mine—it was basically like looking in the mirror.

I SAID, "You have slammed your *last* door!"

216

. . .

WITH EVERY SCREW I REMOVED, it was therapy to my soul. Each hinge had three screws, and there were three hinges on the door. So I had a lot of screws to remove, which gave us plenty of time to drum up some more vile exchanges.

YES, I was bickering with a four year old. Save your judgment. We're all crazy, sometimes!

ANYWAY, I removed the door which caused my little darling to act even more like his momma.

BRU WORKED second shift at the time, so I had to wake him up and tell him to do something with his son.

MAYBE NOT MY most shining moment . . .

SOOOOOO, now we had *three* Brudnicki's who were mad as a hatter!

WE WERE HUDDLED around the kitchen table. Tyler was talking; I was talking; and Bru was about to kill us both. He pointed out the fact that Tyler was four years old. I birthed that child. It wasn't the time for a math lesson!

BRU WAS mid-sentence when he addressed the elephant in the room. "And *where* is his door!" *That* was not a question. He was two seconds shy of a full-blown stroke, at that point.

. . .

It was 'bout to get worse.

His nostrils flared out the size of dinner plates when he spotted the screws and the screwdriver on the counter. "And *why* didn't you pop the pins *instead* of taking out the screws!"

I think I saw a blood vessel pop at this point . . .

I tried to explain the therapeutic action of removing those screws— all nine of them.

That day, Bru wasn't impressed with my parenting style *or* my problem-solving skills.

And that, my friends, is how it all went down that day that three Brudnicki's lost their shiz over slamming doors, removing doors, and — well, all that other stuff that don't paint me in such an endearing light!

Tyler goes on to elaborate on this story . . .

He said that one day, when we were taking a nap, he woke up before I did. He said that he decided he was gonna put his door back up. I had it propped up against the window seat on his bedroom floor.

He said he got down there and tried to hoist the door up. Only, it was too heavy and pinned him to the floor.

In his memory, he was trapped down there for three years. At least. But I was no absentee mom. He couldn't have been down there more than twelve months. Tops.

I JOKE!

HE SAID that he yelled for me to help him, but I was sound asleep and didn't hear it.

God love. I seemed to have had a bad run of motherhood during that time.

And you know what? Sometimes we do.

THE DOOR'S on the frame now. So, at some point, we gave it back. It's all good.

100

MOUNTAIN MEDICINE

When I was little, my Uncle Fred made his own cough syrup. The ingredients were moonshine and honey. When we kids were sick and had a cough, that was the medicine we were given. That's the medicine Hurricane Creek kids in our family had always been given for generations.

Mom tells a story of when I was three years old. She said she gave me a sip of my medicine, then she walked into the kitchen. When she came back into the living room, she heard me sigh a refreshing, "Ahhh." I wiped my mouth on the back of my hand and sat an empty juice glass on the end table. When she had left the room, I dosed myself up with the remainder of the cough syrup.

She said she called Mammaw in a panic. After all, her three-year-old had just knocked back a glass of moonshine. Being that the family had been using it for medicinal purposes for decades, Mammaw wasn't overly concerned.

A small amount of time passed, and the effects were setting in. Mom said I'd stare at the ceiling and just laugh and laugh. Then I went to sleep.

Then I woke up like a sore headed bear.

· · ·

Odd, I still wake up like that everyday . . .

GIVIN' ME THE FEELS

WHEN I WATCH TELEVISION SHOWS LIKE AMERICA'S GOT TALENT, American Idol, or The Voice, I especially enjoy the artists who you can see the angst in their facial expressions, hear the despair in their voices, and watch as their body language conveys an undeniable emotion—whether that be happiness, sadness, pain, or perseverance.

When a musician pours their heart and soul into a performance, as crazy as this sounds, it's like they transfer that energy onto me. I'm an Empath, but I didn't always realize this is why I *felt* songs. I don't have scientific studies to back this up, but I think that's the reason.

When a singer expresses powerful emotion, drawing me into a song—and, by extension, into their world—I *feel* that. I sense jolts of electrical currents that race up and down my legs.

I'm hot blooded by nature. But, in those moments, I feel a chill.

If the performance is exceptionally powerful, sometimes I even cry. That's how deeply I'm connected to music.

SOME OF YOU are laughing at this. And, if this is the case, this passage isn't intended for you.

No, this passage is for those whose eyes just grew a little wider, whose mouth gaped open in understanding, and for those who just bit back a smile while saying, "Me, too."

I DON'T KNOW if this is a result of having a sensitive soul, creative expressiveness, or maybe both. But I can't help but think it's all interlinked.

All I know is that I didn't even realize this was a thing until just recently. Sometimes when something has always been your norm, you don't even realize it's a thing.

IT'S A THING. Feeling music is a thing. It even has a name, frisson.

BUT WHEN MUSIC makes you cry, I don't know what that's called.

OH, wait. I do.

IT'S CALLED the good stuff . . .

102

THE DUMPLIN'S

WHEN BRU AND I FIRST GOT MARRIED, I WASN'T EXACTLY LITTLE MISS Suzi homemaker. I did try, though. My meals were hit and miss, more miss than I care to admit. To this day, he falls into the fetal position if I mention making beef stroganoff.

Anyway, after so many ill attempts at cooking, I finally made chicken and dumplin's that turned out right. They were pretty tasty. In my quest to duplicate that success, I failed miserably, scorching the dumplin's to the bottom of the cooker. While cleaning the kitchen, I had the idea that I would flush the ruined meal down the toilet to get rid of it. That didn't go over so great. The toilet backed up, dumping water everywhere.

Bru went to buy a shop vac, while I was left attempting to do whatever I could to remedy the situation before we flooded the apartment below us.

I did the only thing I could do. I pulled on some gloves and tried my best to free the clog. Now, imagine a dumplin'—the size and shape. Got that picture in your head? I'll just end this story like this.

"PLEASE, GOD. LET THIS BE A DUMPLIN'!"

. . .

THOSE ARE the words I repeated over and over. And over again. Luckily, they were. We freed the clog. And, yes, flooded the apartment below us. She thought our bathtub had leaked. We let her think that.

In years to follow, I still had dumplin' woes. We jokingly referred to me as a culinary wizard because I performed the disappearing dumplin' trick with every pot of chicken and dumplin's. I attempted. We renamed the meal "thick gravy chicken."

Now, after nearly twenty years of marriage, I'm proud to say that I've finally mastered chicken and dumplin's—for the most part.

Hmm . . . Maybe I should attempt that beef stroganoff again . . .

103

THE CARWASH

When I was little, my uncle Jerry worked at a gas station in Berea. It had the first drive thru carwash I'd ever seen.

Curious how I reacted? Allow me to paint a little picture.

You know how you toss paper into a shredder, and the metal teeth grabs it, pulling it down until every last bit is chomped? Now, imagine yourself teetering on the edge of that same shredder. You know how terrifying that would be and how you'd react to that? Well, that was *this* hillbilly's reaction to her first automated carwash. I handled that new discovery like a white-knuckled caveman!

Not only was it loud in there, when the spinning tube came at us—aka, the shredder—I just knew we were toast! Then, long strips of soapy fabric completely swallowed up the car like a row of demented funhouse streamers.

There was the roar in the bay from the scrubbers, *howls* of despair from me, and darkness that closed in on the windows like some sort of plague that was bordering on biblical proportions!

Miranda Lambert said it best when she sang, "It all just seemed so good the way we had it. Back before everything became *Automatic . . .*" I wholeheartedly would have supported that claim, had this song been out way back when.

You can take a girl out of the holler, but when you put her in an automated carwash for the first time, you cannot take the holler out of the girl.

104

THE OAK TREE

THERE ARE PEOPLE, PLACES, AND THINGS THAT LEAVE YOU WITH LASTING memories, imprints on your heart. For me, the Oak Tree is one of those things. In the heart of Appalachia, surrounded by a bountiful forest, one tree stood out.

Everyone on Hurricane Creek was familiar with the Oak Tree. For generations, it had been a meeting spot, a leaning post, and one of the boundaries we were given as children. We could play between the wide spot and the Oak Tree. We didn't have to ask which ones. It was understood—the wide spot below Uncle Ben's and the Oak Tree at the mouth of Preacher's Fork.

A few years ago, during a lightning storm, the tree took a direct hit. News of our beloved landmark coming down spread like wildfire. And, as silly as it sounds, we all mourned the loss.

In the heart of Appalachia, surrounded by a bountiful forest, the tree that stands out the most is the tree that no longer stands . . . The Oak Tree.

** UPDATE: Years after our beloved Oak Tree fell, a Hurricane Creek neighbor, who's a woodworker, gave us all a phenomenal surprise.

He'd had the insight to get some of the wood after the lightning strike. He'd go on to make bowls, vases, and ink pens from the ruins.

I'm proud to say that a piece of this Oak Tree is still with me today in the form of a wooden vase that Billy Ward Pennington made. I would say that he'll never know how much I cherish it. But, he's a Hurricane Creeker; he knows full good and well exactly how special all these treasures are to us all!

105

THE PRESSURE COOKER

THERE'S MANY THINGS THAT TAKE US BACK TO ANOTHER TIME - A certain smell, sight, sound . . .

For me the sound of a pressure cooker coming up to pressure, causing the little weight on top to jiggle and hiss, takes me back to Hurricane Creek and to the kitchens of my Mammaw and Granny.

One of the things we had for supper last night was green beans. When the cooker came up to pressure, and I heard that sweet sound, I couldn't help but smile.

My grannies are no longer with us, so I welcome those little journeys. If only for a little while . . .

106

WASHING BEANS

WHEN MY SISTER AND I WERE LITTLE, WE WERE HELPING MAMMAW WITH the beans one day. They were the good ones - Greasy Beans - and there were lots of 'em!

After the stringing and breaking were done, we were tasked with washing them. I guess Mammaw thought we'd done this before and offered no instruction. Having washed dishes more times than we could count, we asked for no guidance.

So, we filled the sink with our garden treasures, squirted dish-washing liquid *all* over them, added water, then sloshed them around until they were good and soapy!

I still remember the shrieks of despair when Mammaw came into the kitchen and saw her little darlins' washing the beans . . . with a sink full of suds!

She scooped those beans up in a pan and pitched them over the porch rail. It took a few trips, and we stayed far away for fear she'd pitch us, too.

This little memory came back to me today as I was washing beans . . . And it sure made me smile.

107

THE WATERFALL

SEPTEMBER 23, 2018

WHEN I WAS in the first grade, Mrs. Roark read a story to the class that has stuck with me my entire life. Well, one scene from it, anyway. In the story, these kids kept their milk cold by keeping it in a waterfall. That scene stood out to me.

OVER THE YEARS, I've thought of that story and often wondered what book it came from. I did an internet search recently and discovered that it was The Boxcar Children.

OVER THE WEEKEND, I went to a bookstore with my friend, Jill. I looked and looked for the story, to no avail. As I turned to leave, I turned back and reached up on the top shelf to select a book from the series. Any book. Something was better than nothing. Right?

· · ·

ABOUT AN HOUR AGO, I was flipping through the book and discovered that the book I "settled" for is the *very* book that has the story I was seeking.

SO TONIGHT, this forty-five year old woman will read a story from a children's book with all the excitement and wide-eyed wonder of a first grader. I am ecstatic!

108

TRIALS OF A WOMAN

I WALK OUT TO THE MAILBOX,
    And find a card inside,
    I wonder what it is,
    And, then I nearly die!

AN INVITATION TO A WEDDING,
    I really shouldn't care,
    No one will be looking at me,
    But, whatever shall I wear?

I GO SHOPPING,
    For just the perfect dress,
    But soon realize,
    That this is just a mess.

I SEE THINGS I LIKE,
    And, then I find my size,

And, then I try it on,
And, then I want to cry!

THIS PLUS SIZE GAL,
is faced with some problems,
Hoo-chi-mamma short skirts,
or a pair of bellbottoms.

MY OPTIONS ARE QUICKLY FADING,
It accentuates what it shouldn't,
I wanted something new,
But, realized that I couldn't.

I TEAR THROUGH MY CLOSET,
That doesn't help one bit,
Nothing I want to wear,
Or, nothing that will fit!

I FIND MYSELF SOME SPANX,
That'll do the trick,
But they just push the fat roll south,
Now, I'm feeling sick!

SO, I put on the girdle panties,
Maybe this will help,
Now I have a bigger problem,
I've created a muffin shelf!

THE SPANX PUSHED IT DOWN,

And, the panties pushed it up,
Now, my fat roll is front and center,
Like an obedient pup.

WHATEVER SHALL I DO?
Whatever shall I wear?
Who came up with these torture devices?
It's really too much to bear!

I'M DRESSED LIKE ELVIRA,
To this summer wedding,
Black from head to toe,
Something to be dreadin'.

JUNE NUPTIALS ARE GREAT,
I gave it my best shot,
I can't wait till it's over,
. . . cause I'm really HOT!

~ *Amy Pennington Brudnicki*

109

THE WIZARD OF OZ

WE WENT TO THE LAND OF OZ FOR OUR JOURNEY WITH DORTHY. THE Wizard of Oz is my favorite movie of all time, so I was *super* excited about this trip!

TYLER HAD a big test that day but was able to reschedule to go with us.

So, Bru, Tyler, Emily, and I headed off to North Carolina on our quest to see the Wizard.

SOMETIMES AUDIENCE MEMBERS are chosen to play certain parts. Being that I wouldn't fit in Dorothy's costume *or* her shoes, I was thrilled to be chosen to play the part of Glenda, the Good Witch, and even more excited that Tyler was cast in the part of the Cowardly Lion—who he insists on calling Tigger.

· · ·

WE WERE able to go inside Dorothy's house, which was an unexpected surprise, but super cool. We saw the house before the tornado and after. Outside the front door was our world. Just beyond the back door was the Wicked Witch of the East, the ruby slippers, and the yellow brick road.

I WAS INSTRUCTED to stand on a pink pedestal platform where I was able to lead the crowd in a spirited rendition of "Ding, Dong, the witch is dead." Dorothy insisted on helping me sing. Where's a flyin' monkey or falling house when you need one!

I had some more dialog with Dorothy, then, we set off on our journey to follow the yellow brick road . . .

WHEN IT CAME time for Tyler's part, he was able to jump out on the crowd where he roared, "RAWR!" And, "Put 'em up! Put 'em up!" He continued on with his iconic lines, as did the Tin Man, the Scarecrow, and the Wicked Witch of the West.

ONCE WE MADE our way to the great and powerful Wizard of Oz, the Tin Man got his heart, the Scarecrow got his brain, my Cowardly Lion got his courage, and us witches got a sticker that said, "Maybe I was Good. Maybe I was Wicked."

DOROTHY ENDED our journey by clicking her heels together three times, all the while repeating, "There's no place like home. There's no place like home. There's no place like home."

I LOVED every second of this trip. It's not very often that you can step inside one of your favorite movie sets and have the opportunity to reenact the scenes.

. . .

My favorite part of all was being able to share this experience with my family.

AND, now Tyler has a new phrase. Since our trip, he's been saying, "Glenda, honey, listen . . ."

110

HANNIBAL

BEFORE THERE WAS HANNIBAL THE CANNIBAL FROM SILENCE OF THE Lambs, there was an equally horrifying Hannibal that struck terror in the hearts of many. Hannibal was a dastardly goose that my cousin, Tommy, had. It was summertime on Hurricane Creek, and I was about to be served a helping of humble pie . . .

My cousin, Micha, was up in the holler behind Mammaw's house. She called and said she was afraid to come home because there was a goose up there. Well, this was before I knew anything about that man eating goose named Hannibal who was waiting to unleash his reign of terror on me. So, her sister and I trekked up the hill to rescue her. We passed Tommy's house and walked on to Larry's where Micha was waiting. She said she was afraid to go get her bike because the goose was over there. Well, being that I wasn't afraid of a goose, I walked over and got her bike for her. It was a cute little girly bike with a big fat horn and everything. I gave it a little "honk honk" and walked back to Larry's house to gather my cousins.

Andrea, Micha, and I walked past the goose, past Tommy's house, and were approaching the hill when something told me to turn around. I've learned that when God whispers to you, you should listen. Soooo, I turned around and saw this goose waddling down the hill behind us. I told it to go away, but all I saw was waddle, waddle, waddle . . . I'd walk a few more steps, turn around, and there it was. Waddle, waddle, waddle. I would scream at him to go home. Still, here he came. So, I did the only thing that made sense to me at the time. I threw a rock at Hannibal – not meaning to hit him, just to get his attention.

WELL, I certainly did get his attention, and then he got mine real quick!

EVEN THOUGH I didn't hit him with the rock, apparently I did make him angry.

Think back to the Bugs Bunny cartoons where they show the birds flying through the air like fighter pilots in the war. Well, Hannibal, the dastardly goose, was about to wage war on me! When I looked back once again, he was coming at me, running at me like lightning with his head down low. My God that thing could run fast! I impressed myself that day because I was running so fast, I was about to take flight.

THIS WAS a prelude of things to come.

WHEN MICHA SAW that crazy goose, she took off. She had an advantage. Her little girly bike blazed a trail right in front of us. So, there we were – Andrea, me, and a very, *very* angry goose! Andrea and I realized that this goose meant business, so we decided to take off running faster. HA! That dumb goose was about to eat dirt. I knew we could run faster than he could. Off we went. I have never ran so fast for time to stand *so* still in all my life. Andrea and I were screaming for our lives!

From my house, my dogs could see that something was terribly wrong with me. They were going crazy. Mom came out on the porch to see what the fuss was all about. In the distance, she saw us running and flailing our arms. She concluded that a bee was after us. It was one *big* bee! So she turned and walked back inside! Thanks, Mom!

REMEMBER THE PHRASE, "WHEN PIGS FLY?" Well, that would be surprising, wouldn't it? For a pig to fly, I mean, chickens can flap around. Ducks can fly. We all know that birds can fly, but what Andrea and I did *not* know was that geese could also fly! We turned around, and this man eating beast was coming at us, head down, fighter pilot style. He was hissing – *hissing*! What an awful sound. But, then we saw something that nearly made us both die, on the spot! Not only was that hissing creature coming at us fast, his feet were *not* on the ground. *That thing was flying*! Oh, my God! It was flying! We were so about to die!

As Andrea and I ran for our lives, we still had quite a ways to go. When we reached the bottom of the hill, we had to cross a bridge that covered the creek below and still had to run some more to get to anyone's house. Luckily, we were kin to everyone in our path, so the first house we came to is where we were going. It happened to be my Uncle Eddie's house.

Andrea and I were running side by side and throwing out ideas as we went. I'd look to the left and toss out an idea. She'd look to the right and toss one back. It's amazing that we could even understand each other. We devised a plan to escape our impending death. We decided that once we got to the bridge, we were jumping off, and the goose would keep right on flying. Then I played this idea out in my head. I could see me jumping, her jumping, and being that neither of us could walk on water, we surely would have met our maker because that deranged goose would have held us under the water until we struggled no more. So, we quickly canned that ingenious plan. I don't know if Hannibal got faster, or if I blocked out my near death experience, because the next thing that I recall, we were in my Uncle's yard. I remember being near the bottom of the hill, but not crossing the bridge. So anyway, we were now, somehow, in my Uncle's yard. At this point, Hannibal was between Andrea and me. Low and behold, she took off.

THANKS, Andrea!

So, here I was battling this beast of nature all by myself. I looked around and saw my uncle's car. It was locked, of course. So I decided to climb on top of the car. Here came Hannibal. He was going to get on it with me. He wasn't hissing anymore, so that was good. He was back to waddling around, but I wasn't about to fall for the "innocent goose" routine. You never know when you go trusting something and then it starts flying on you! I was not falling for that! So, I ran around trying to decide what to do. My uncle wasn't home, of course, and his house was locked up tight, of course. *But*, as I walked around the house, I spotted my way out of this predicament. There was a ladder leading right on top of the house. I had begun to climb the ladder when I played that little scenario out in my head and foresaw that unforgiving piece of fowl getting up on the house with me and tossing me to a very painful landing. I quickly saw that this was not the best of ideas, so I scurried down the ladder and ran to a little building that was around the side of the house. Now, let me remind you that I would *never* have entered this snake den if I were in my right mind. But, I guess all the excitement of the flying goose had me a bit addled! I was in there with God only knows what. But, I did have a door that halfway shut, so I was somewhat sheltered from the hissing, flying beast! As I stood there and pondered my next move, I saw Andrea. She hadn't abandoned me after all. She had gone and fetched herself a tree. Yes, a tree! I assume the idea was to get a big stick to protect herself with. Well, she did. She found an enormous tree branch, and up the driveway she came with it. She was ready to face Hannibal when I saw Tommy's wife, Maggie, drive down the road. I heard her say, "Here, Hannibal." She called that dastardly goose like a dog. *Like a dog!* And, it came. There she went up the road, and there that goose went right behind her. It was flying after that little gray car like that was a normal thing! This is when we realized that Micha hadn't abandoned us, either. When she took off on her little girly bike and blazed that trail in front of us, she went straight to our Uncle Eb's house and called for backup. Andrea and I thought that Micha was kicked back eating ice cream and playing video games at home, but she was actually saving our lives! That day, God was on our side—and getting a big laugh, I'm sure!

So, on this seemingly normal summer day, I learned some valuable life lessons. I am, *indeed* afraid of geese. And *never,* under *any* circumstances, blow a little girly horn from a bike when you are near a goose. It's either a mating call or highly offensive to them. Either way, that outcome is not good for you.

AND, they can fly.

GEESE. CAN. FLY!

LORD HAVE MERCY ON SILLY PEOPLE, GEESE CAN FLY!

IN CONCLUSION, before there was Hannibal the Cannibal from Silence of the Lambs, there was Hannibal, the flying, hissing, possibly in the mood for *love*, dastardly goose that put the fear of God into three little girls one summer day on Hurricane Creek.

111

I FINALLY DID IT!

THERE'S A SONG WHOSE TITLE POSES A RATHER PROFOUND QUESTION: "When was the last time you did something for the first time?" As it pertains to this entry, June 29, 2018 is my answer. On that day, I published my debut novel, Vanished, by Amelia Blake. Amelia Blake is the pen name I use when I write fiction.

LET ME BACK UP . . .

I STARTED WRITING VANISHED on a crisp October day. It took me nine months to write the book. Many more crisp days, and a whole slew of Octobers came and went before I was satisfied with the manuscript. In total, it took six years to write, re-write, edit, add, omit, *and* finally get the courage to submit my story.

PEOPLE WOULD SAY, "HAVE SOME CONFIDENCE!" Or, they'd sometimes say, "Just publish it, already!" The truth is, it wasn't ready. And neither was I. No one knew who I was or what I was capable of as a writer.

That included me. I'll never regret waiting because it gave me time to hone my skill and shape my story until it was right.

PICTURE THE WRITING process much like you would that of a robust southern cook making a pot of vegetable soup. She doesn't just throw some ingredients together and hope for the best. No, she adds her ingredients, her seasonings, she stirs, tastes, cooks, simmers, and tastes some more. She likely adds more seasoning until it's right. Once it simmers a bit, she gets a better idea of how it will taste. And, if needed, she tweaks it a few more times. Storylines are no different. Sometimes, you just gotta let something sit a bit, and go back to it. You'll know when it's right, whether *it* is vegetable soup or your very first novel.

OK, back out of the kitchen and back to the story . . .

IT TAKES a lot of courage to send your work out into the world. Back when I started this process, I was so afraid of what people would think. My book is a steamy romantic suspense. It consumed me to think that I'd let my family, friends, and community down, or they'd somehow be disappointed in me. On the night of the final edit, I realized what I'd achieved in writing "my little story." I finally believed in myself as a writer. Suddenly, that took precedence over what anyone else may or may not like. I liked it. A lot. After all the revisions, I still laughed at silly parts, cried over emotions that my characters felt, felt dread when I knew something bad was coming, and I cared about my characters. Still. I felt their emotions, still. And, in my closing scene, I visualized them. And when I wrote the words, "The End," it wasn't the end because I mourned the loss because their story was over. If it could make me feel all that after six years, I thought, just maybe others would feel that way, too.

. . .

THAT LATE NIGHT IN JUNE, I decided it was ready, and I was ready.

THAT NIGHT, I called Bru and Tyler into the living room because I wanted to share that special moment with them. I put my laptop on the table, and we all gathered round - one of them on each side of me. I asked them to place their index fingers on mine. With a million emotions coursing through me, I blew out a shaky breath. They say if it scares you a little, that's when you know it's right! On my cue, we all pressed down at the same time. Pressing the button together, we published my debut novel.

I HAVE RECEIVED countless messages about my book. I've had people say it was therapeutic for them. I've had a few that had negative things to say, but luckily, not that many. I'm proud of my book, and I'm proud that among the fiction, my readers could find things to apply to their lives to make a situation a little easier.

I THANK God for giving me the ability to be a storyteller. I'm not much of a speaker, but I can type a story. My gift may be different that yours. That doesn't diminish either of our abilities.

IF YOU HAVE A DREAM, chase it. There are plenty of people who are quick to tell you all the reasons you *can't* do something. Those are their fears speaking. That is not *your* truth. Surround yourself with people who see your worth and will remind you of your capabilities. And, in turn, be the person that does the same for them.

LOVE AND LIGHT,
   amy

112

WE ALL SHINE IN OUR OWN TIME

January 30, 2019

I had a thought cross my mind yesterday . . .

When I was in elementary school, we would sometimes take field trips to the library in town. Being that our school was close by, the teachers would line us up and walk us over there.

At that time, the late seventies, the library was set up with a little reading nook to the right as you walked in. The small bookcases were positioned in a rectangular shape, a perfect layout for little ones to wander into and find an age appropriate book. I don't remember which books I looked through, read, or had read to me, but I do remember the smell of the books. If you're a "book person," you'll understand this. I also remember the sound and feel of the plastic that covered the wide rectangular storybooks.

· · ·

My memory comes from the perspective of my little child self. I can remember sitting on the floor with my back to the bookcase that backed up to the library entrance. I remember looking up and seeing a book displayed to the left above the top shelf of the nook. The book was Humpty Dumpty. I remember clearly seeing that little egg-shaped fella sitting high atop a brick wall. I don't have an exceptional story to follow that up with, just that I remember the book. I'm guessing I would have rather been hearing that story than whatever book was being read to us.

A few months back, I stopped by my little hometown library one early morning on my way back out of town. As I walked through the doors, the smell of library books hit me. I was immediately transported back in time. I couldn't wait to go inside and wander around that little reading nook. As happens with time, things looked a little different inside. The little nook was no longer there. I was lugging around a box of books, so I didn't go in search of it. I'll definitely do that next time.

Anyway, the thought that hit me yesterday was this: my hometown library, the one that I went to as a child for children's books and as a teen for research assignments, that little Leslie County Public Library now houses *my* book, the book I wrote under my pen name— Vanished, by Amelia Blake. I have a great sense of pride in knowing that.

I never really excelled in school. I got by, but I didn't excel. I wasn't a fast reader. To me, that always meant I wasn't smart. Somehow, I wish the adult me could have settled in beside the child me. Maybe as *little me* glanced up at that Humpty Dumpty book, the *grown-up me* could've whispered in her ear that it was ok to not be the fastest reader, that one day *we* would have a book of our own in that library, that we all shine in our own time.

MAYBE I DID HAVE an exceptional story to follow that up with after all.
. .

113

ONE FINAL THOUGHT: PRESERVING HISTORY

CONSIDER, FOR A MOMENT, THE STORIES THAT FILL UP YOUR MEMORY bank. I hope you have a vast collection. I know I do. Growing up in southeastern Kentucky in the seventies and eighties provided me with a great many tales. My brother, sister, and I played all day, and we played outside. Some kids today think that's surely an Urban Legend. But we did. Along with a whole slew of cousins, we made mud pies, climbed mountains, rode bikes, waded the creek, went sleigh riding, sang Christmas Carols, rode the propane tank like a horse, and played basketball. We roamed Hurricane Creek. Our boundaries were from the Oak Tree to the wide spot, and we didn't go beyond them . . . *much*. And we were always home by dark. No streetlights and no sidewalks for us. Dusk was our "streetlight," and a well-worn dirt road was our path.

Typical country kid stuff. And, when we got bored, we did it all again—except for the winter stuff. Neighbors just think you're weird if you go singing Christmas Carols on their porch in the summertime.

I no longer live in southeastern Kentucky, but the experiences I gained there helped shape me and will not be forgotten—not by me nor by my family. The only way to assure that happens is to preserve history by recording it. My stories are written. My hope is that, through my retelling of life on Hurricane Creek, my child and big city husband will have a better understanding of what it was like to grow up in a rural community.

But I do have regrets. In 2014, my little Mammaw left this earth and with her went many wonderful unrecorded stories. You see, Alzheimer's Disease locked her memories long before she passed on.

Please, don't wait. The time is now. You don't have to be a skilled writer or an eloquently spoken individual to preserve history. You just need to jot down some questions and ask them. All you need is patience and topics of conversation. Sometime down the road, you'll thank yourself. I can promise you that. Once your loved ones are gone, either physically or mentally, so, too, are your opportunities to ask the things you've always wanted to know . . .

The memories that stand out the most in life are the ones made extraordinary by everyday occurrences.

~ Amy Pennington Brudnicki

A NOTE FROM THE AUTHOR

I hope you've enjoyed my shenanigans and stroll down memory lane. I've certainly enjoyed reliving the stories.

In case you're wondering, every word is true. That's what makes a lot of these stories so incredibly funny to me—the windshield wipers, the Slap-A-Ho Tribe, America's Most Wanted . . . all true.

Mull that over for a moment.

"You can't make this stuff up!" That's a phrase I use often. And, with stories like mine, why would I dare add to them?

My hope is that if you have an old soul like mine, that you'll be inspired to tell your own stories. You just never know who'd love to hear them.

Thank you for your purchase. If you enjoyed Echoes of the Past: My Dirt Road Diary, please consider leaving a review. It doesn't have to be anything elaborate, just a few words. You could even say something about your favorite chapter or simply state the chapter title. It would be interesting to read which entries connected most with readers.

Reviews help encourage others to take a closer look at an author's work. They're appreciated more than you know.

Thanks for taking the time to read the stories about my life. It's been an enjoyable trip back to yesteryear . . .

~Amy

ACKNOWLEDGMENTS

I'd like to thank these amazing people who have helped me along my journey to publish this book—some of you helped in ways you won't even remember.

To Miss Emily Eckert—or Emmaleah, as I like to call you—thank you for the help with the picture.

To Audrey Clowers, my forever BFF, thank you for a lifetime of memories. There's so many stories I had to leave out of this book. Soooo many! I love you great big, my boo.

Thank you for brainstorming with me, for encouraging me, and always having words of wisdom. You're a wise old soul, and I appreciate you more than you'll ever know.

To Elbert Estep, my very wise and dear friend, thank you for helping me convert my photo. It seemed to be lost forever between incompatible computers. Without it, I may have never published this book—that's how strongly I believed in it gracing the cover!

To my friend, Jill VanDyke, I want to say thank you. For many years, you've encouraged me to continue writing and even compared my writing style to that of a famous author. You told me that you could see my stories. That's the highest praise that any writer can receive. Thank you, friend. I appreciate you!

Jeanna Cornett, you've been a wealth of information to me. Thank you for the advice and guidance.

Miranda McDaniel, I thank you for being a sounding board for me. I appreciate it more than you know.

Karen Valentine Wells, I appreciate your help with ironing out the details that my memory was a little fuzzy on.

Sherry Cheak Eaves and Brian Eaves, thanks for the help and words of encouragement. I appreciate you both!

To Jane Young, my dear friend, I'd like to thank you. For many years now, you've encouraged me to keep writing and to publish. You knew the importance of chasing my dreams. Thank you for always being so supportive.

Holly McCreary Tussey, I think you'll be shocked to see your name here. Many years ago, I was answering a quiz that asked what I'd most like to do. I answered that I'd like to publish a book, but I didn't know how.

You said that was no excuse because I could get a book that told me how!

I laughed at that, but that advice has stuck with me all these years. Thanks for the nudge.

To Bob Lovett and Martin Pemberton, thank you both for the encouragement early on. I think you both saw something in me that I didn't see in myself. Thanks for the push.

To my Aunt Meff, you said something to me one day in a voicemail that I've never forgotten. You said, "I love you, and I love what you do. Keep it up!" I could hear the smile in your voice as you said it. I could tell that I brought you happiness in that moment, and in turn, you brought me joy with that statement. I just want to say thank you.

Katharyne Shelton and Isaac Gonzalez, I want to say thank you to you both. Last year, I stumbled into a group that I thought would teach me marketing. It taught me so much more than that! Through your tutorials, I gained the courage to at least attempt to design a book cover myself.

This book is the most personal thing I've ever put out, so I'm eternally grateful to you both for creating a group—KDP Amazon Kindle Self Publishing With Katharyne, Isaac & Tangent Templates—that gave me the knowledge and the courage to create a book cover.

To everyone listed in this book, I want you to know that this is more than me just rambling off names. If you were mentioned, it's because you've left an imprint on my heart, and I want you to know that I'm grateful for you and the memories we've shared.

To my friends and family not mentioned in this book, y'all know I love you. There's a million other stories I could have written—some of y'all better be glad I *didn't* write a story about you! I mean that as a joke, and I hope you're smiling.

To my shovel crew, my Forks, my midnight disposal posse, The Dance Confessions at the absolute worst time *ever*, and any other inside joke I couldn't write about, thanks for the memories . . .

ABOUT THE AUTHOR

Amy Pennington Brudnicki was born and raised in Hyden, a quaint town in southeastern Kentucky. At an early age, she penned clandestine paranormal mysteries—nothing more than a page in length—and always quickly discarded. As a forlorn teen, she began to write poetry. Her collection was stored in a ratty old notebook and tucked away out of sight.

Throughout her life, she wrote tales that would evoke laughter in anyone who read them. This was all before the age of the Internet. Shortly after high school, Amy's home was destroyed by fire. She and her family lost everything they had, stories and poems included.

Thinking that writing was nothing more than a hobby, she laid her pen aside and focused on her education and starting a family. Years later, her old soul caught up with her as she felt that familiar pull once more. She has since written newspaper articles, a novel—Vanished, by Amelia Blake—and this collection of short stories, Echoes of the Past: My Dirt Road Diary.

Her purpose in sharing this with you is to urge you not to give up on your dreams. She'd tell you that it's never too late to dream a new dream, just as it's never too late to explore one previously set aside.

In the powerful words of Aerosmith, "Dream on. Dream on. Dream until your dreams come true."

I love my readers. Give me a chance to read about *your* shenanigans. Add me on facebook!

f

ALSO BY AMY PENNINGTON BRUDNICKI

AMY USES A VARIETY OF PEN NAMES WHEN SHE WRITES OTHER GENRES—AMELIA BLAKE IS HER PSEUDONYM WHEN SHE WRITES FICTION, AND OLD SOUL PUBLICATIONS IS THE AUTHOR NAME FOR HER GUIDED JOURNALS. THE SOLE PURPOSE OF THIS IS TO DIFFERENTIATE BETWEEN WRITING STYLES. FAMILY MEMORIES BY OLD SOUL PUBLICATIONS IS A GUIDED QUESTIONNAIRE JOURNAL TO HELP PRESERVE FAMILY HISTORY. VANISHED BY AMELIA BLAKE IS A STEAMY ROMANTIC SUSPENSE.

Vanished

Family Memories: A Guided Questionnaire Journal to Preserve Family History

Book 3

Made in the USA
Columbia, SC
20 September 2019